Published by Lift Bridge Publishing

Copyright © 2016 by Dominique D Jones

All Rights Reserved

Library of Congress Cataloging-in-Publication Data

Jones, Dominique D

Shattered my Silence

ISBN 978-0-692-61889-9

PRINTED IN THE UNITED STATES OF AMERICA

FIRST EDITION

THE REASON THIS BOOK DOESN'T HAVE ANY CHAPTERS BECAUSE IT'S MEANT FOR MY READERS TO JUST GO WITH THE FLOW. I DIDN'T HAVE TIME TO STOP, TAKE A BREAK IN MY LIFE AND REFLECT ON IT SO YOU WILL FEEL EVERYTHING I EVER FELT…ARE YOU READY? TAKE A DEEP BREATH AND JOIN ME ON THIS JOURNEY OF MY LIFE

Today I am taking my heart, soul and everything in me through so many different emotions but I need to tell the story of my life. Who am I? What makes me different from others to just sit and write my 1st autobiography and think that it's going to get into the awesome, God blessed hands of Tyler Perry? I AM HER VOICE, I AM HER CRY, HER LAUGHTER, and HER PAIN…I AM DOMINIQUE

DANYELL JONES a little girl with so much pain, a woman with heartache, a voice and determination to make her life known by others. To let them know they can get through that struggle and live life with a purpose and a testimony to encourage others.

Day 1 ...Jan 20, 14 10:59pm

Lost, then found my way…My Story, My Song, My Testimony

Today the Angels sang a beautiful song!!

Dominique Danyell Jones, was born on February 19, 1976 to Carl Jones Sr. whose 7yrs senior to my biological mother. I'm born not knowing what my life had in store for me. Not knowing my feelings of who was in front of me or what life I was dealt with but I live. From this point here I was told what happen in my life because I had no recollection of my past thus far back. No one in my family knew of me until I was 3 days old. I have no clue why I was actually taken from my mother at 3 days old but I was told it was best for me by my family and later on in my adult life my mother.

    My father was in the army and on leave at home when I was born. So, before he went back in the army and was stationed somewhere he took me from my mother out of the hospital and brought me to my Grandparents (my angels) his parents to give me life and raise me. I was told 1 day my father came to my grandparents' home and knocked on the door late night. My grandmother looked out the window to see who was knocking and my grandfather asked who's at the door. My grandmother said it was Carl. So my grandparents came down stairs and my aunts did also and all peaked around the corner to see what was going on. My grandmother opened the door and right away told my father to come into the house.

    Not knowing what was wrong she insisted for him to come first and then to ask questions later. My father then said to my grandparents that he need their help. My grandmother said sure but asked him what is wrong. No one ever paid attention to the army coat that he had in his hands because of course he was in the army. He then walked up to my grandmother while she sat down and placed the coat in her lap. My aunts then came down stairs and stood around my grandmother to see what was going on.

My grandmother started unwrapping the coat that was placed in her lap and there I was. A very tiny light bright (very light in complexion) infant. A beautiful little baby girl with a full head of coal black curly hair. Everyone was confused about who baby I was and why am I here. So my father told my grandparents that I was his child by this young lady and that he needed them to raise me while he was away in the army. Of course they accepted and my father was ready to leave out.

My grandmother insisted that my father stay that night but he left the house that night.

My grandparents then took me upstairs to their room. They put me in the middle of their bed (I took my youngest aunt place lol)... Aunt Nadine and from that day, was the best day of my life cause I was placed with angels that would care for me, love me, take care of me, respect me and most important Give me to God and raise me to know who he is.

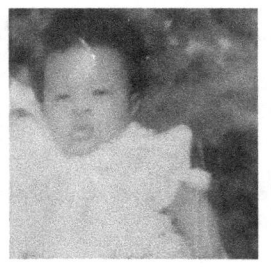

POEM TO MY FATHER

I was brought into this world as a peaceful, beautiful little girl.

Not having a care but with my little eyes I did stare, coming into this mixed up crazy world.

Held close to my father, and him knowing I was his daughter.

Knowing I needed to be cared for and we headed to the open door.

My best interest at heart you know I needed, so you took me to whom you knew couldn't be defeated.

You wanted me to have the best because you were headed to war, giving your 3 day old daughter to your parents to raise and care for.

Thank you for loving me the way that you did,

I was your child, little girl, your only kid.

You don't really know that you mean a lot to me, and it may have been some time for you to actually see.

You were always in my heart and this is where you will always be.

A love that can't be explained

It was like I was made just for my grandparents. I say that because of the bond that we had together. I could talk to them about any and everything without a problem. I could listen to their thoughts and advice and take it into strive. I was brought up to love God, pray to God and go to church every Sunday morning, Sunday evening, Monday evening, Thursday evening every week. I knew when it was time to put on those panty hose (that use to make my legs itch) heehee it was time to get on that bus and head to the big church on the hill.

I love going to church because I would see everyone greeting everyone with hugs, the smiles that lite up everyone faces made me feel so happy inside. When you hear my pastor voice come across the microphone singing (ohhhhhh yeaaaa, thank you Jesus, amen and praise him) I just knew Yes, this is it! The lights come up and I know it is worship time. You hear the praising of the congregation and the singing from the pastor and his wife then the choir. It was like fresh breath of faith into my lungs and heart that carried me through the week. Growing up in a household with my grandparents and their kids (9kids) but some left the house early but still came around.

It actually felt like I was the little sister to my Aunts but no matter what I kept the respect and called them Aunt at all times. I was a spoiled brat and I knew it. Today 12/22/14 I have sat with my Aunt Nadine and we talk a lot and she told me that she loved me to death.

Just at one point at a very young age she use to give me the mean mug (laughing my butt off). She said that I would ask her do she want to play and she would say "NO" with the mean mug.

She said for some reason I didn't see that she was mean mugging me. I'm so innocent at this age and coming in taking over her spot I do understand but she said she wouldn't let anyone hurt me. My Aunt wanted me there but she will give me that mean mug a lot. She noticed that I wasn't paying attention to her or didn't understand what she was doing so she stopped giving me the "mean mug". I was soooo spoiled by all. I didn't have to lift a finger to do anything. Even when I got older in my teens to cook, clean, wash a dish…anything and everything was done by my Grandparents and my Aunts/sisters and they loved it (heehee).

They spoiled me because they loved me

and they felt what I was going through enough even when I had no clue. I know that they all made me into this little princess diva that loved all of them more than they ever knew. I love my Aunts! Aunt Nadine, Aunt Felita, Aunt Rita, Aunt Evon, Aunt Maxine, Aunt Sylvia & Aunt Diania! I rarely got to see my Uncle Buck because he went away to the army as well as my father at a young age. As a little girl I was always watching and admiring what was going on around me. I was very quiet and shy if I didn't know you but more just very laid back and observant.

 My grandmother was a praying woman and I knew her and God was the best of friends so I did what I knew was best by listening to her and she became my very best friend. So I watched how she would walk, I watched her talk, I watched how she brushed her hair, how she brushed her teeth, the songs she sang when she would get up early in the morning. I admired my grandmother and she was my hero. I wanted to be just like my mom (grandmother) how she took care of everyone around her and not one time at all have I seen my Grandmother complain for any reason or cry unless she was praying and talking to God. She would wake up extra early in the morning and make breakfast for Granddad and everyone.

Granddad was also up early in the morning either in the kitchen with Grandma while she cooks and straighten up or getting himself ready for work. The morning normally started with Grandma singing those great hymns or gospel songs and everyone smelling the great scents of all the food kissing your nose. I always said "this is the life and I want this forever". As soon as I would come down the stairs and around the corner from the living room, whoever saw me first would greet me with the most heartfelt smiles and a beautiful sound of "good morning Nique". The smile and love that I felt was astronomical from them. I thought this was going to be for the rest of my life but I wasn't thinking about one day I will be growing up and either moving out on my own or having kids of my own.

I just knew that I would have my 2 best friends with me for the rest of my life. I'm not saying everything was perfect because I saw a lot of things go one around me. No family is perfect but this is what I felt. I felt like I played the little boy in the movie "Soul Food" that for some reason all situations played out around me and I couldn't do anything but carry it in my heart. I saw my Aunts getting hurt mentally and physically by the love of their lives (men). I had an Aunt that was dragged down the street and beat up on in front of people and she's trying to get away but ended up staying with this man (the hold that we let love have on us).

I had a family member that for some odd reason put his hands on his lady. I saw that so much or even hearing that this was happening again my heart started getting cold for this person. Also, I had another Aunt that loved a man and he just took from her but she gave him everything and he gave her nothing but heartbreak because he chose drugs instead of being her backbone. She was the best woman a man could ask for. Yes, she stayed with him and why you may ask??? Her heart was in the right place in having a family, love and forever but his mind was into drugs (she eventually left him though).

I also had an Aunt that was murdered by her boyfriend in front of her daughter. Her boyfriend was very jealous and abusive. He said that if he can't have her no one will. I never remember meeting this Aunt but my family always talked about her. So much had played out in front of my eyes and all I could do was cry inside for everyone. My grandmother would pray all the time and all I heard was my grandfather yelling and cursing out these men for hurting his girls.

His heart was hurt and no one knew but I sat by my granddad one time and he cried hard because his heart felt all the pain his kids was going through. I cried too but I was young and I just wanted everyone to be happy like when we would go to church and we would see all the happy smiling faces that would come up and give hugs. I just wanted everyone to get together in one place and just have God come in and take away everyone's pain. I don't know if I ever really took a deep breath to let out something/everything that I held in for everyone. My grandma always prayed for everything no matter what so I felt that genuine love and affection that just oozed from her soul. Man she was an awesome lady and I knew that no one had a person in their life like I did.

I was blessed and I didn't want to share my grandparents with anyone. I remember as a little girl my biological mother use to come to my grandmother's home and try to take me from them (blackmail). She didn't want me just what she could get from my grandparents (bribing them) for money. My father couldn't do anything because he was stationed somewhere in the world. At this time my grandparents only had temporary custody of me. So that meant since my biological father wasn't here the next parent had all rights to take me.

    She was dealing with a lot of things so some people isn't stronger than others. Drugs and Alcohol started becoming apart of her life. If she didn't have money she would come to my Grandparents home and threaten to take me unless they would give her money. Plenty of times they would give her money but first they would try to get her to stay with them and feed her or whatever so she would just stay there with them. No, she didn't want that. I was told that on a few occasions I almost passed away because of her carelessness. I was very young and on one occasion she had me (younger than 11 months old) on the back of a motorcycle with a man driving and it was very hot outside. I was very dehydrated and she didn't know.

    She called my grandparents up and said something was wrong with me and she didn't know what. They came and picked me up and took me to the hospital right away. The doctors said it was good that I came in when I did because I wouldn't made it through the night. On another occasion where she had me at her home she decided to have a house party. They had drinks all around. I was told that I was rushed to the hospital where she didn't know any information on me and had to wait until my grandparents to arrive so they could give the doctors info to help me. The doctors then said to them I was so drunk if I wouldn't have made it there in another hour I would've been dead.

She also stated on another occasion that so she can leave out of her house for a few hours she would put a little alcohol in my bottle so I would pass out and sleep until she come back in. Can you imagine someone giving alcohol to a baby to just knock her out so she can run the streets? It was said that my lip was shaking so bad as if I was cold but I was so drunk. That was the last day that she came to take me from my grandparents' home. Anytime that she came before and brought police when she came my parents had no choice but to let me go because they didn't have full custody of me per my biological father. I didn't say she wouldn't stop trying.

My grandparents fought as best as they could to keep me safe but the next to the last time was when she called the police on my parents because they wasn't letting me go with her. The police came and outside they told my biological mother that she didn't have the right to take me and if they had to come back they would lock her up (she was drunk). Then the officers came into my parents' home and told them what they just told her but actually she can come and take me so they advised them to get the right paperwork done so that if she tried again she wouldn't be successful. They got in touch with my father and he put papers through where my grandparents had full custody of me for a period of time so when he came home he could take me back if he wanted to. Oh she tried again for sure because she wanted that money. It's a shame that my grandparents had to put money aside like they were paying an extra bill for my biological mother.

So when she would come to try to take me she knew that they would give their all to just keep me home and safe and she then would take the money and leave. So, one day she came through and my grandma wasn't home yet from work. I knew as soon as I saw her or heard her voice I would take off and run heart pounding hoping she wouldn't find me in the house. So this day I was ready for bed in my night pajamas just happy. I was about 5yrs old and a knock came upon our door. It could've been anyone but my heart started to pound so hard that I thought everyone heard it.

    It's sad whenever you hear a knock on the door of your home (where you supposed to be safe) you just feel danger. My grandfather looked at me and said "nique, it's alright. You are safe here with me and momma". He went to the door and asked "who is it". A voice spoke "It's me wheezy". I instantly felt like I was going to throw up. I begged granddad not to open the door but granddad said I would be fine.

    So he opened it. She asked granddad "where is my daughter? I'm taking her with me if you don't have any money for me". My grandfather said "wait until momma get home, she's on her way". She didn't want to wait and I peeked around the corner and she saw me. I was so scared and I didn't want to go with her at all. She started coming close to me and my Aunt grabbed her and told her no she isn't taking me. So her and my aunt started to fight and my aunt had her on the bottom of the stairs against the closet door (I was happy) because I knew she couldn't get me if she was on the ground and couldn't get up.

So the fight was broken up by another aunt and my granddad but my mother wouldn't stop. So my granddad had to sit her in his chair and sit on her lap so she would have to wait until my grandma came home. A few minutes later Grandma came in the house and saw what was going on and told her that she can't keep doing this to me and them. She has to leave and she's not getting any more money. My grandparents wanted my mother to be a part of my life but anytime I would go with my mother something bad would have happen to me. Once my biological mother also had to call my grandparents to come to the hospital because I was in her care and wasn't responding. She didn't know anything about me to tell the doctors.

When my grandparents and some Aunt's arrived to the hospital giving the doctors information about me once again. They found out that I had alcohol poison. I was so drunk again and I was under the age of 5 at this time. I almost died then. Don't ask me why the doctors or police didn't see that she was unfit to care for me and only wanted money. God definitely was with me at all times because I had a praying grandmother, grandfather and lots of family. On another occasion my biological mother called the police on my grandparents and said that they wouldn't give me to her so the police did take me out my home and place me in the hands of a woman I barely knew.

That day I was with her she had all these people in her home drinking and doing other things. After a while everyone started to leave and she told me that she will be right back just sit in this room upstairs and be very quiet. I was in a room that was dirty with 2 little kids that I didn't know but she said watch them. They were my little brothers and much younger than me. I was very quiet but I wanted to go home with my parents (grandma and granddad). They were all I knew and if I was in there presence I was safe.

All I had to see my Aunts faces and I felt complete but sitting in that dark room with 2 babies and didn't know what to do cause one was crying and I tried to console him. I wanted him to be quiet because I didn't want to die if someone was to find us. I just kept saying it's alright to both but wasn't sure if they understood me. I didn't know why we was in a room and was told to be very quiet, I thought she was hiding us so someone wouldn't get us. All of a sudden I heard this banging on the back door down stairs. The banging wouldn't stop and this man was yelling my biological mother's name.

So this man bust in the house and started calling my name. He was my biological mother's brother and he was very upset that she left us alone in a house. He grabbed us up and then I remember being back with my angels in my home…..my safety never felt complete. I just know as a little girl and growing up all I knew was safety was with my grandparents because God lived in them so I knew I was good cause who would mess with a child of God. My Aunts have told me that from when they could remember I was covered in Jesus name.

They just knew that something was different about me but just didn't know what it was. At one time I was told that I was very little sitting on the couch and above my head hanging on the wall was this very heavy picture. You know those pictures that has that frame that bulges out and very heavy to pick up?

Blessed beyond what I ever knew by GOD

So I was just sitting there and the picture fell off the wall but no one could get to me in time and God knew that. So, when it fell off the wall everyone said that it should've hit me in my head but it looked as God just smacked it to the side and it went flying the opposite way. Tell me that wasn't God! That's why my aunts said that I was covered by God and it was something about me that was special. My little life seemed as though I was always hiding in fear or running from my mother. So from me running trying to hide from my biological mother or scared that she's coming to take me with her, to seeing my aunties going through hard times with men, to seeing my grandmother praying over bad situations and my granddad hurt was the bad part for me from the ages of 8 and younger.

But, the best part was being in such a happy home filled with love and most of all God. No, every family isn't perfect and neither was ours but they were my family that loved everyone and helped out anyone so that's where I received having a heart of Gold and filled with God. I had the best family a little girl could ask for and I knew I was blessed but I was missing something and didn't know what. One minute I would be happy and smiling and the next minute I would be crying and don't know why I was so upset. My grandma always knew what to say to make me feel a little better. It was the tone in her voice, the look in her eyes, the love in her heart, and God sitting beside her when she said "Nique, pray and give it to God!!!

She knew I was hurt and sad but they did everything right that they were supposed to do to raise me. I was deprived of not being able to call out or say out of my mouth "Mom or Dad". My grandparents told me plenty of times that I can call them mom and dad but even though I loved them more than anyone could imagine it didn't feel right to do so. I don't know why because they were just that to me and more. I never got to call my parents mom or dad when I saw them because I didn't feel it. If I needed to get their attention I would just start talking to them or say something that would make them turn towards me. I rarely saw my biological mother with many years going by and I learned of her last name in my late 20's.

So, when grandma told me to pray, I did exactly that but I never knew what she really meant at a young age by that because she always said "me and daddy is here for you always". But, everything was pray and give it to God. So I did! I knew as a little girl how to pray because I mimicked my grandmother and like I said her and God was best friends. My grandmother would talk to God as if he was sitting right beside her and he was listening to her every breath. Praying was easy for me but what I needed was to feel the safety from the physical cause the mental wasn't there. So much was going on in my young life that when I was scared I could run and hide under my grandma.

    Just hearing when my grandmother talk in such a pleasant way and composure but at this time I just knew in my grandma was the physical that I needed but not until my teenage years I knew God was talking through her. I should've fell in love with God but I fell in love with my grandparents because all these years it was God talking through them. I just saw them and felt there hugs…. (All along it was God and my grandparents letting God use them). So at the age of 9 is when I knew I was safe and my biological mother couldn't steal me anymore or come and get me. I felt that I could let down my guard and actually be a little girl and not worry that if I would go outside she would be watching me from around the corner to grab me and I wouldn't see my parents anymore. I FELT SAFE! That was very short lived when my biological father came back into the states and I don't know how I really felt about that. Just because I didn't want him to try and take me with him.

    He came back with a woman and he told everyone that she was his wife. He told my grandparents that he was going off to Germany and they were happy for him until he said he wanted to take me with him. Why did he say that??? I remember he was telling me that he was taking me with him and I said "oh no you're not, I'm staying here". Just because he was my biological father didn't mean anything to me. He had the whole house upset because he asked my grandmother can she pack up my things.

I saw my grandmother in my room and she was pretending to get my clothes together but she was going very slowly so that he may just change his mind. He didn't know that he was killing a part of my grandparents and myself very slowly inside. I tried to hide in the bathroom, I was screaming grandma please help me!! Don't let him take me!! Please, I was begging and crying and screaming but all I saw her do was hold her head down (she was crying)....I know he was killing her inside.

My grandmother told him that I didn't have to go but he wanted me to not seeing what it was in the best interest for me. I didn't see granddad in the house cause I was looking for him but I was grabbing on everything to get him to see that I really didn't want to go. So when my biological father reached the door with me I knew it was over for me and he would get me into his car. So getting to the house door and outside I saw my granddad telling him to just leave me here (with a stern voice). Granddad was very upset and my biological father getting upset because everyone wants him to leave me but he wants me to go with him and try and make a family with these people I knew nothing about. He wasn't going for that and I yelled to granddad to pull my arm and keep me here.

I'm yelling "Help me granddad, don't let him take me please help me". My grandfather was so upset and I saw him shake his head in anger. I knew that was going to be it for me. My biological father gets me in the car but I'm fighting and he locks the door so I can't jump out. I watched my grandparents' house door 1810 Richfield dr to see if my grandma would come running out and I watched my granddad watch me until we couldn't see each other again. At that moment I didn't know I wouldn't see them for another 2yrs.

    Leaving that day out of my neighborhood all I could do is think of a way to jump out of the car. I didn't care if I would hurt myself jumping out of the car as long as I would see my parents again is all I wanted. My biological father was running late to get to the airport because my grandmother was taking a long time to get my clothes together. I didn't know until years later that my grandmother stopped talking that day and a whole month went by before she started talking again. She also had a slight heart attack from the pain of me leaving. Granddad was very sad and hurt also.

    This situation tore them up inside. My family lost their little Nique and my aunties I missed so much that quick. So, I left for Germany with nothing to my possession. My father didn't mind buying everything that I needed so he was rushing to get to the airport but was pulled over by a cop. I want to say so bad…"help me please, he kidnapped me from my parents" but I was scared the police wouldn't believe me and I didn't want to get into trouble by lying. I wanted to hit him in the back of the head and knock him out so that he would fall out but I didn't want to get into a car accident and get hurt myself.

    In the car was my father, his wife and her son. They were looking at me and I was rolling my eyes. I wanted to be the meanest little girl but instead I just ignored them and wouldn't talk or eat. We ended up staying at the airport waiting for the airplane that would take us to get on the army airplane nothing like a regular airplane to take us to our destination. I missed my parents and my Aunts and cousins so much and I would say their names all the time so that I wouldn't forget anyone. I didn't have any pictures of anyone. I just had a very good imagination so I would just sit all alone on many different occasions and talk to them and tell them what I was going through.

ANOTHER WORLD TO ME

    This may be why I'm a very visual person now. Getting to Germany was a different world to me. They were speaking a different language. I was being taught in school over there German but I declined because I was being very stubborn. Friends I made there were German and I had to communicate with them. That's the only reason I ended up learning it. I just wouldn't speak it around my father because I didn't want him to think I like it there.

    I loved Maryland and the English language so I wouldn't give up with what I believed in cause I wanted to go back home where I belong. I stop eating so that he would just give up and send me back home on a plane. He didn't give in. When I left Maryland I was a thick little girl (chubby) lol. My biological father tried everything to get me to eat but I said I rather die if I couldn't get back home. So I was getting very hungry but I started to eat cinnamon graham crackers and cheese (that's it). That's the only thing I would eat for a very long time but then I started to eat because I was getting very then and was told that I would go into the hospital if I didn't eat.

I didn't want that because again I knew that I wouldn't get home to my family.

POEM
IN GERMANY I PRAY

Lost little girl in this different type of world

Not knowing who to turn to, not knowing who to trust

I sit and cry that I no longer mattered, feeling no more than just a grain of dust.

Can someone just help me? God, you said you loved me

Feeling so invisible, can anyone hear my voice? Can anyone just see?

I'm hurting inside! I just want to die! If I could be a bird I could just fly.

Just fly away in the air is where my heart would stay

I just want to be free from this pain inside of me

If I could just die I would live in the clouds and be the angel I was meant to be

Or maybe I could find my home and be forever with happiness

Instead of here crying, and feeling nothing but my heart's sadness

It has to get better one day. I sit and pray that

somebody would just say. "I love you and I want you here" "I would take your heart and all of your fears".

I would go to bed at night just hoping that God would take me with him that would be my life, my story, just my end!

Now, while I was in Germany I met some good people that came into my life. In my apartment building it was 2 different families that I was introduced to and the introduction with one family was me being taking into their apartment and them just watching me while my father did his normal at that time. Going to the bar across the street or maybe just being in our apartment. I really don't know what was going on but I remember being down stairs in this young white or German couple place. They kept their place dark or with minimum low lighting. They didn't have doors, instead it was beads hanging down from the doorway.

    They seemed to be more like a hippy couple and but with a great heart. I remember one day being in the tub looking out into the hallway and just hearing the lady asking me am I alright and am I finished bathing. The guy (her husband) never came around unless I was fully clothed. God was with me when I had no clue because I didn't know them and they didn't know me. Anything could've happened to me. At this time my biological father and his wife that came with us to Germany separated.

    One day I remember I was sitting in the living room and my biological father wasn't there. I was sitting in front of the television playing a video game "frogger" I was so addicted to this game lol. I was in the house with chickenpox so it wasn't much for me to do. So, all of a sudden the young couple that watched me on plenty of occasions now told me to close my eyes and they have a surprise for me.

One said I'll be right back and I heard the door shut. Then I heard the door open and close again.

He came up to our apartment sat a coat down on the floor and I watched it because it started to move. I was scared a little but they told me there's nothing to be afraid of. So all of a sudden this long rat thing ran out of it….. did I jump up and run like fire was on my butt lol…I sure did! I never saw anything like this before in my life it was called a "Ferret". It was a very harmless animal but it was a cool pet. They wanted to give it to me but I still was pretty much scared of it so I didn't take it.

Then my biological father came in the apartment with a house full of friends. Wherever he went people just gravitated to him. He was a good person in heart but I didn't know him well enough to go with him to another world (to me that's what it felt like). I wanted the young couple to take me with them to their apartment but I couldn't because I was dealing with chickenpox but they told my biological father that they would take me anyway. He said no they can leave and he thanked them but the whole time I was staring at them walking toward the door. They were watching me also and then they waved goodbye.

    I could tell they loved me in a way of caring and I felt safe with them. I actually wanted them to adopt me because I didn't feel safe with the lifestyle my biological father was living. I didn't feel stable in his household. So, like I normally do is just watch and make sure my surroundings are safe by not having my back towards anyone. All these people would come around and talk to me and I would just sit and listen but all was running through my mind was that I wanted to go home where I belong. I remember when the young couple were moving out the apartment I felt so lost and I cried and they wanted to take me but they knew that they couldn't.

They both cried and apologize to me for leaving but they had to move. I don't remember their names or really what they look at this time but they're in my heart for being such great and wonderful people that I kept them in my mind all these years. So, next was a family that live upstairs and they were a black family with kids. They took me in whenever my father went across the street to the bar that we could actually see from our apartment. My biological father did take care of me physically like (keeping me clean, going shopping all of the time, I had all the latest games, clothes and going to swimming parks). He was trying to spoil me but I was so lost without my family back home.

He tried his best but just because of the situation with him being in the army, left him to give me to his parents and me growing up not knowing him. He made sure I was straight with my grandparents with sending money without them asking. He really appreciated my grandparents for keeping me safe and raising me. It was just he was still a single man that really didn't know how to be a father just yet. The family that would watch me whenever my father went out took good care of me. They were very nice people but I think what took the cake is when one day a tragedy happen.

    My biological father left the apartment and headed to the bar across the street and I was in the apartment above with the new family and we all smelled smoke. The father and mother went out in the hallway and ran back in the apartment. They were yelling hurry and get your shoes on everyone. They stated that it's a fire in our apartment and my father isn't in there. They got everyone out of the apartment and someone ran to the bar and got my biological father. The fire truck came and they put out the fire that was in the kitchen.

You could see the kitchen and the fire from outside the apartment building. My biological father forgot that he put a pot of beans on the stove, left the apartment and went to the bar directly across the street from our apartment. That was one of many crazy times in Germany I had to deal with. I had a few times where it was kind of cool to be able to learn some German, meeting new people and actually travel to another place. I felt that my family was going to forget about me and I didn't want them to do that. I just didn't feel loved and complete over there.

    A 9 yr. old girl moved to Germany with her biological father, his wife and one of her sons. They were trying to make a family that I didn't want to be a part of. I already had a family that they took me away from and I knew I would never forgive him for that. At the age of 9 I already saw, heard and been through so much that I knew I was different and wasn't sure where I would go from there. Where would God take me because all my prayers still didn't get me back into the hands of my family that loved me and best as possible kept me from danger, pain and hurt. So, I use to ask myself what's next for me.

Where is this life going to lead me because I'm scared and I need to feel safe? Please God Please God come get me and take me back home.

So, here's is what was next in my life...

While in Germany my father and his wife separated and her son and her moved into another apartment and she basically moved on. My father didn't want that but it wasn't anything he could do. One day we went over to her apartment and he thought he heard another man talking to her and he got very upset and he wanted her to open the door. She didn't and kept telling him to leave. I was just standing there and didn't know what to do. I didn't want to be there and wanted to leave so bad but he wanted to get into her apartment. He ended up bursting into her place and a little tussle begin with him just trying to get the phone away from her (he didn't put his hands on her).

    She was on the line with another man talking about my father. After a quick min he just said "come on Dominique, she's just not worth it and from there I felt hurt and pain from him and for him. I just watched him walking toward the car and in the car I watched him until we went back to our apartment. That year in Germany was a very long year. I don't know why but he said to me that I'm going with his ex-wife to her family home and he will be coming to get me. I didn't know why he just didn't want me to go back home with my family. I was a 10 yr. old little girl that stopped eating so that he would just give in and send me home.

He didn't though and I thought about everything in the book to get back home but nothing ever helped to get me home. I saw so much in Germany and it was a learning experience for me but it would've been better that I didn't go through it. I looked at my father in a way that I wish I didn't. I hated him, I didn't like him. Now you know how I felt when he told me that he's sending me with my stepmother and her family to Arkansas. I didn't want to go with people I knew nothing about. I just met his wife the day that he took me from my parents' home in Severn, Maryland.

I knew nothing about her and I didn't try to get to know her. I didn't talk for a very long time and that's when I also stop eating and then tried to commit suicide. I wanted him to see that I wasn't doing well with him and he would give in and just send me back home. Being pushed to another state with people I had no idea who they were or what they would do to me was the worst. Now, I'm traveling to Arkansas and I get to this little house that looked kind of spooky. I had no say in where I was going or coming I just had to shut my mouth and obey these old people.

After we arrived to Arkansas my step-mother left me and her son with her mother and for a whole year I didn't see or hear from her. So, why did they even bring me there? I thought these people was supposed to just get rid of my body and I would never see my parent's again in life. I remember getting out of the car for the first time, grabbing my bags and walking on a dirt walk-way to the side door where you had to enter the house. The screen door was loud when you opened it and needed some paint work done. I guess they didn't think that I had manners so they were saying aww you're so cute and whenever they gave me a compliment I would say "thank you".

They would say aww and she has manners. I would say "Yes ma'am, my grandparents taught me to have respect for everyone and my manners just come naturally". I don't know again why I was there but I had no choice but to make the best of it. If I tried not to talk or eat I would be scared to know what they would give me if I tried that. We had to go to church every Sunday morning but that was it. They weren't really nice people but they couldn't be to mean because I had very well manners and obeyed them.

One day I was told to go to the top of the hill where this very old couple lived and the place was really run down. I was told to go up there and take them something (I just don't remember what). So walking up the hill and

I was thinking of my family back home and looking down this very long road that looked to lead to nowhere. I was wondering if I was just to run and never come back would I eventually find my way back home or would the police locate my family because I knew my address. The lady that I was staying with would tell me all the time that my family didn't want me that's why I'm there with her.

    I didn't want to believe that but I said "my father may not want me but my grandparents do and if they knew where I was they would be here to pick me up". Walking to this old couple home and reaching the door. I knocked and was told to come in. The house was a mess but I took them whatever it was that I was told to bring. The older lady talked to me a bit and said "baby, you are a really sweet little girl". I said "thank you"! She said come into the kitchen with me for a minute. I did!

She talked with me a bit and said "I don't know why (she named the lady I was staying with) would want to send you to a girls home. You seem to have the sweetest heart and so nice. At that moment my heart started pounding and I said to myself "I'm never going to see my family again and tears came to my eyes. I thought that I would have to kill everyone so they wouldn't send me away so that my family wouldn't find me. So a few minutes later that lady came to the house and walked in. She said what's going on?

What are y'all talking about? So the older lady said "I don't know why you would send this precious child to a girl's home". The lady said what else would I do with her? Why don't you keep her then? The older lady said "I would but I can't care for me or my husband now. I'm sitting here listening to them talk as if I'm not here debating where I was going.

So the older lady said "take care of this

child"! The lady said goodbye to me and I walked out the house with the lady. I didn't know my next move but I knew that I needed to get out of that house before they killed me. So the next day I planned this in my head that I would go outside like I'm playing and just run away. So all the kids were told to go outside and play for a while. We all did but I did what I normally do and just walk up and down the dirt road leading to the main road.

So the kids decided to go see a baseball game that normally happen around there but it was a walk down the road and through the woods. So I thought here's my time to run. So I walked with the kids and let them get ahead of me. They started down this road and we walked for about maybe 20 minutes and disappeared into the woods. When I saw the last kid go into the woods I started running and running. I was all alone on the road that seems it was going nowhere but at that time I didn't care.

    I just didn't want to be in that house anymore because I didn't want to go into a girl's home and I didn't do anything to anybody. As I'm running this car passed me but then started to slow down and back up. That scared the mess out of me and all I could think of was being murdered and really I didn't know if it was better being kidnapped by someone else or going back to this house. When the car started backing up I turned toward the way I was running away from and ran back to find the kids I ran away from. While I was running pass the car I heard the voice from the car asking me am I alright but I just kept running and finally found the opening in the woods. So scared and hoping the person in the car wouldn't find me I hurried up and sat on these bleachers with people that was watching the baseball game.

    I sat and watched the game thinking "what am I going to do"? My mind was in deep thought and I heard all this yelling and people running towards me. I was confused like what's going on. This lady grabbed my leg and said are you alright? I said yes why? She said "the ball was just hit over the fence and hit you in your knee and it was really hard.

   I didn't feel anything until I actually stood to my feet to walk away and was in pain. They offered to take me to my house but I told them I didn't live here just visiting. I said "I am fine! It doesn't hurt that bad" but it really did. I ended up walking back to this house that I didn't want to go to but it was better than being on the scary streets alone. I was at this house for a year and when that lady give me the news that my father called and he sent me a plane ticket to come back to Maryland I knew I would be safe back in the arms of many that loved me so dearly. That day came and I didn't care to pack anything I just wanted to actually get to the airport and get away from these people.

Getting in the car I was so excited. We stared driving off then I thought to myself. This lady is going to take me to this girl's home and leave me. My smile turned into a straight face and I started asking questions. ME: Did my father say he's coming to this airport to pick me up? Her answer: No, he's waiting at the other airport with your aunts

ME: Can I see my ticket? Her answer: You have to wait until we get to the airport

Now I'm thinking in my head…Do I have to grab this wheel and kill all of us because they are not taking me to a girls home. I started looking out the window to see if we were headed to the airport and I saw Welcome to (I forgot the name of the airport). My smile was there again. Man when they stopped and opened the door so I could get out it was like I could breathe again. I never looked back to goodbye or anything my focus was on getting home to my parents and my family. Getting on the airplane I was so excited and I was told that my father and my aunts was waiting for me.

They had a stewardess ready and waiting to take care of me the whole flight. She did just that and didn't leave my side until I recognized my family. I already was upset with my father because he sent me away with these people that didn't make me feel happy at all inside and the only time I was a little happy is going to church because it reminded me of my grandmother. The songs, the hugs and smiles but the lady that I was staying with would be a very happy person at church but when we got back to her house it was more like everyone upsets her. I tried to make her smile and happy but it wasn't much I could do. I just wanted to be home with my family where I knew for a fact how much love they had from me and knew everyone was safe myself. I worried about them so knowing that I was on my way home made my heart lighter than ever.

Home never felt so good

So getting off the airplane, and walking through the little hallway to see everyone that was waiting for the people to come off was exciting. I knew I didn't care to see my father and was looking for familiar faces.

I did and I ran hugged them so tight. The fly attendance that was taking care of me on the airplane asked me did I see anyone that I noticed. I yell yes and thank you as I ran to my family. My father was there but I never saw him. I think I actually blocked him from my thoughts and from the time he pulled me away from my family and me going back into their arms was 2 years later. It was such a blessing but my family asked me when they saw me for the first time getting off the airplane.

"Nique, is that you"? I said yes with a little grin. They said "where did my Nique go"? My weight was gone and I was very tiny. I was a thick little girl getting spoiled rotten and eating all the time and never having to clean I was a real true life princess. I laughed and said "I know! I stopped eating but I never told anyone what I went through in Germany and in Arkansas. I kept all of that bottled inside for all these years.

So, driving up the street that I was familiar with made me so happy. I watched the door until we parked and got out the car. The excitement and anticipation of seeing my grandparents and all my family was what I cannot put into words. So walking into the house it was really quite and I didn't know why. I thought that my family was going to jump out and surprise me but My Aunt told me to go out the back door. So I followed my family out the back door and so many people was out back. They were having a cookout and I saw kids I never saw before because my Aunts was pregnant when I left. I started walking out the door and I saw 2 beautiful little girls walking together and they were only about 2 years old. They both looked like tiny porcelain dolls.

One was very light skinned with hazel eyes and so tiny (Tierra). She looked like she wasn't supposed to be walking yet and the other was the most gorgeous little girl that was dark skinned (Sharita) and the biggest eyes but she looked so fake because she was so gorgeous. I wanted to pick them up so bad and they just watched me as I was oohing all over them. Straight faces the whole time I was talking to them and when I started to walk away to find my grandmother, I turned to look back at them and they were smiling at me while I was walking away and I thought that was so cute. So I walked into my Aunt Rita's fence where everyone was sitting around and everyone was yelling, calling my name I felt like that princess again. I felt right at home and I was finally home. They held me like they never wanted me to leave their site ever again.

I use to have the most beautiful days back home because I actually could touch my family and not having to imagine what they look like. I missed my grandparents so much I would wake up in the middle of the night and go in there room and get in the bed with them. My grandmother would move over to the middle and I would lay on the end. My grandfather never said "go back to your room" He knew that I needed to be close and that was the only time I actually felt safe. I could hear early in the morning my grandmother waking up singing her gospel and I could never forget her voice and that awesome smell of breakfast that she still cooked. I didn't hear granddad say much but I could smell his cologne and I would never forget that smell.

We lived in Severn, Maryland a neighborhood called Pioneer City. My grandparents was well known by all because their hearts was of Gold and they accepted anyone and everyone and also took care of all. My grandfather use to have this electric guitar and he would hook it up to this amplifier that would be so loud you could hear it all round the neighborhood and everyone knew that was my grandfather Arthur William Jones Sr. He would bring that electric guitar out and that big old speaker right on the side of our townhouse and you hear this loud noise before he start playing that good ole music. Granddad had talent and he was a very strong minded man with a huge heart and love for others, even the people he didn't know but a very strict man. We lived in Richfield for about 11years in the same home the whole entire time.

That home I had so many emotions and feelings from fear, to love, to happiness, fear, to concern. Many birthdays which every year it would be the same thing. I would be at my Aunts home up the street and then someone would come to get me and bring me home. I would get out the car and someone would tell me that something was forgotten in the car and I would be the one left outside alone to get it and me racing to get to the house quickly. I would get to the house and it is dark inside. I would open the door and say "grandma, granddad…" and no one would answer but I have 1 foot outside the door and 1 foot inside the door.

Then all of a sudden everyone would pop up and scream "Happy Birthday Nique". My heart would be pounding out of the chest but I was so happy and so blessed that I have a family that loved me so much. We eventually moved down the street to our home off of Pioneer Drive and we would do so much in this home. So with this moving we actually walked our things down to the other house. Who moved with us to the house? It was who was living with us the time before.

It was my Granddad, Grandma and my Aunt Evon and her daughter (my teen teen). She had 1 child at this time that I would hold a special place so close to my heart and said I would look after her my whole life like my little sister (teen teen). Then my Aunt brought my little cousin into this world and now I had a little brother (Dave). I couldn't wait to get home. He would be sitting there in my Aunt's arms or when he got bigger he was on the candy truck with my grandmother and my Aunt. He would turn around when you call his name and stare at you with those big beautiful eyes.

It was amazing having 2 other little ones running around the house with me and I didn't feel jealous with them. I remember the day my Aunt went into labor with her daughter in Richfield Dr. She was laying on the couch in labor and I didn't want to leave her but I had to go to school. I was so excited when I got home she was already gone to the hospital and soon I would meet my little cousin. When she finally came home I would watch her as her little fingers would move, when she opened her eyes I wanted her to see me first. I would get very close to her to smell her cause she smelled so good (like a newborn baby but I didn't know what that smell was back then).

    I adored her so much and still do! So eventually we would move down on Pioneer Dr. and none of our routines changed except my granddad not hooking up and playing his electric guitar. My grandparents came up with a plan to have a candy house and they did so. It eventually became a candy truck which everyone in the whole neighborhood would come to and get candy. My grandparents would give kids free candy or chips for no reason most of the time. Everyone knew my granddad as the strict Mr. Jones but they also knew that he had their best interest at heart.

Granddad would come out early in the morning and get the truck together before the school kids would come out to catch the bus and grandma in the house preparing our breakfast. Granddad would be out there 3 different times in the morning because he had the high school kids first, then the middle school kids an last the elementary school kids. I would watch him opening the truck from our bathroom window just to make sure he was safe on it and locked in. Everyone loved Mr. & Mrs. Jones and I was so jealous because I wanted them all to myself. That tiny bit of selfish came from me being pulled away and me not wanting to leave them again and anyone taking them from me. My grandparents also had the people during the day that came to the house at any time for something on the candy truck and my grandparents would go out and service them.

We had drug dealers, to drug users and

just about anyone come to that truck and my grandfather would say in a stern voice "hey you need to get yourself together and get off these streets! Are you hungry? Go in the house and tell Momma get you something to eat! It didn't matter who it was my grandparents was feeding anyone. Anyone would be thinking all these strangers coming in and out of this house wasn't safe. My grandparents put trust in God first but never had fear only losing someone that they loved and they loved all. It was there heart that was in the right place and God blessing them to be able to help others. I know as soon as I use to get off from school I would run to the truck not knowing which of my grandparents I would see.

    I would look around the door and peak in the little window. Both of their smiles had me smiling so much bigger and they would both say "Hey Nique, how was school? Come and get a snack and go in and get something to eat. I would sit on the candy truck for a little while and talk to them and then eventually go in the house and do my homework. Then in the evening when it was time to lock the truck up I would go out and help and everyone would get there snacks for the night and go inside. Granddad would talk about the day with grandma and I would listen. They never talked about anyone bad just how they wish they could help them.

 Every day was the same routine with my grandparents. So growing up with them in the house was fun and they always came to my room or I would go in my Aunt room so that I could play with her kids. My Aunt kids would come into my room also but man they loved watching the Disney movies or cartoons on VHS. They had every single movie that just came out oh and knew every song that was sung (I only knew because of them lol). My little cousin, she had the most beautiful smile and I would always go in their room and she would smile. Either she would be singing those Disney songs with the princess and the Lion king.

Lion king was our favorite movie. You could learn the words really easy because my Aunt had all the Disney movies and they would have the words at the bottom and I would be singing along with the words. We had a lot of fun and still some nights I would go into my grandparent's room in the middle of the night and tap her shoulder. She wouldn't say anything but move over into the middle of the bed and I would climb up beside her in a nice warm spot and fall asleep. My whole entire childhood with my grandparents I didn't know I was actually getting set up for my future and since all I knew was prayer and talking to God and listening to my grandmother. Singing praise songs and seeing her worshiping was molding me into my future.

I was loving God, talking to him and knowing what to do when I felt sadness I would go to my grandma and tell her "I'm mad and I don't know why". She would pray with me but I would listen and let her talk to God for me. I relied on my grandparents for everything and they made sure I didn't want for anything and kept me spoiled. Still never had to lift a finger to clean, cook, wash clothes or anything for myself. I would ask do you need me to help but they always said "no you can go and relax". I would sit around them all the time and listen to stories that they loved telling.

I felt it was fascinating all the stories that they had tucked away in their brains. It was a pleasure to come in the room and listen to stories all day long. I loved my grandparents so much that everything was fascinating coming from them. Just my grandparents being in my life was the best that a hurt, confused, angry at times little girl I could ever ask and pray for.

I did a lot of praying back in Germany and in Arkansas that God would please send me back to my parents and I would never leave there side ever again. I would help them roll coins at night to go to the bank in the morning. They were my rock!

Now me becoming a teenager I had respect for myself, loved God and understood a lot more about him. Doing great in school but still so freaking shy but was known as Dominique the little church girl but it was all in fun because everyone knew me and we all had much respect for one another. I remember when we were young also and my grandma would say "ah you getting on that church bus with me". All my cousins was the crew that always had to go to church no matter what and it didn't matter how tired you was, you was getting on that bus. So when you got to church you knew that grandma was going to lay down her sweater either on the floor or on the chair and you get up there and go to sleep. A little funny that my cousins use to laugh at.

    My grandmother would be sitting there praying and thanking God but she was so tired getting up so early in the morning and going to bed kind of late. She still wouldn't miss a beat in going to church. She would be sitting there with her eyes close rocking back and forth. All of a sudden her head would fall back or forward. She would catch herself and always would say "Thank you JESUS" and when we get home or after service we would be laughing saying "grandma, you was knocked out sleep". She would say "I wasn't sleep! I heard everything the pastor was saying. I was just resting my eyes" and we would laugh because we saw her sleep. Grandma would recite the whole sermon or what the preacher preached and we knew we was wrong but it still was funny.

Becoming a teen (the) "Know it all" & My 1st love

High school was good and my grades was great except my first semester in 9th grade I failed. It was a lot to take in and all the boys that was so handsome had me so distracted. I had so many crushes but never told any of them. I kept it to myself but they all was always around me and my friends. We all pretty much grew up together in the same neighborhoods and still they wouldn't know. I couldn't focus but I surely got myself together and made that up. I remember this guy that I was so attracted to. My first boyfriend and I fell head over heals with him.

He was a so fine and just my type of guy. All I cared about was he choose me to be his girl. He was just gorgeous but I was a tomboy just coming out of hanging with the fellas and showing my girly side. So shy to even talk to him but he was interested in me. His name was Danny Lee! I honestly don't remember how we became boyfriend and girlfriend but everyone knew we were a couple. One day he came to me with a gift. I was so happy and he just didn't know how much he had my heart.

So when I opened it, It was a chain with a pendant that opened like a book and said "I love you" on the outside and the inside it had my birthstone which was seen in the front also. It was very unique and I cherished it because it was from my dude. I wasn't worried about the material things and never was. It was just a beautiful gift from him to me. I still was very shy even with him and he dealt with it. He was and still is a wonderful person period. I wasn't having sex and lol I knew he had. I wasn't giving it up and he never asked or made me feel like I had to. I was just in fear of having sex and still wanted to wait. I was sure he was sexually active, I just wasn't ready.

He was very respectful but I felt that I shouldn't hold him back from that. I wasn't sure myself when I wanted to but I knew it would be when I got married. I wasn't thinking very clear but I kinda let it happen and through the years I still had a huge crush on him and he knew. We grew up and he moved away but not far. Anytime he would come around the way either I saw him and like a weirdo would quickly go the other way (lol don't judge me) or anyone in my family would say to me "guess who I just saw"? I just knew because everyone in my family knew and still to this day know how I felt about Danny.

He came around wanting to see me also but thought I was avoiding him for other reasons (we both were wrong). He's a good friend of mine today and I wish him the best in life.

Growing up and learning my way

Now, everything was good at this time in my life. Every now and again around this time I would see my biological father and he would brag on me to his friends about my accomplishments in school and my goals that I was pursuing. He would tell all his friends "this is my daughter, she's smart and getting all A's in her classes" blah blah blah. I was still upset with him so I wanted to hurt him and I thought I would do it by him always blasting me about me doing great in school and going into college (that was my plan) my future was so bright. No kids, not once thinking about wanting any kids but I loved them. So one day at school the seniors was called down to the library to get sized for our caps and gowns.

Everyone was excited and here we go the teacher called a few students away and said we had to go the guidance office. We all was a little confused to why we aren't out there getting fitted. They told me at the last minute (not when they knew) that I needed a ½ of a credit and I wouldn't walk the stage… I had to go to summer school. Now, I already was a teen with a tiny attitude but now that you are telling me this all late made me angry.

So I yelled at my guidance counselor and left the office. I was supposed to go back with my class but I didn't. I went to the cafeteria where my home girls was on lunch and the assistant principal was guarding the door. He said "you don't belong here Ms. Jones". I said "I know I don't". He then said "where do you belong?" I was done with the questions and wasn't thinking clearly.

I started thinking about a lot of things and just keeping things bottled up had me really upset. The Assistant Principal said "I will call your father"! I looked at him and said F@@% you and him and walked in the cafeteria. I saw my girlfriend, told her I was out I'm leaving and then walked out the side of the school near the front entrance where they had the phone booth. I called my older cousin Lisa to come get me. I told her what I did and she said "you are freaking crazy".

I told her hurry up for someone come and tell me get back in school. She came and I got in the car with her and drove away. I WAS SO STUPID FOR THAT DECISION!!! I never thought that it may make my father feel some kind of way but it was messing up my life but at that time I couldn't think clear I was just so angry. I didn't go right home that day to face my grandparents because I didn't want them to be disappointed in me at all. I came home after school was out but since my grandmother was my best friend I told her everything.

I talked to her that night and she told my grandfather because I asked her to do it for me. We were in for the night and I was anticipating him calling me. Then that voice "Nique, come here! It didn't sound mean but I still didn't want to tell him that I did something so horrible by cursing out the Assistant Principal and then walking out. He just talked to me and said "Momma and I want you to get an education and that wasn't a good decision". You don't have too much time left in school so what we are going to do is keep you home and you start fresh next year.

My mind I was like "oh no"! I ended up saying "Yes Sir" and kept it moving. Granddad said to me also "Don't ever feel afraid to talk to me or momma because we are here for you". I love that man so much! I ended up going to cosmetology school in downtown Baltimore, Md. I was so excited about that because I was into beauty and making others look and feel good about themselves.

I was on my way to becoming the best cosmetologist in the game (so I thought). I would go to cosmetology school every day with a couple of my cousins that was enrolled with me Carlet and Alicia. I started feeling very bad that my grandparents had to put out money every day to send me off to school and I wasn't able to give back. They would always say to me "Nique, we will give our last to you as long as you are doing what your heart is in it for but it has to be in your best interest". That for me wasn't enough to make me feel good inside so I decided to get a job and work then come back to school at a later date.

Living at home with my grandparents I decided to move out and I moved in with a cousin at the age of 18 but often came to visit my grandparents. They never wanted me to leave and said I will always have a home there. I thought that I should try and become a woman because they sheltered me way too much and I was being spoiled way too much. I needed to grow up and be an independent woman (this is what they were teaching me).

My grandparents would always tell me that I could come home anytime I wanted and always asked me did I need money and/or anything.

I would tell them no even if I was in need of anything. I was becoming an independent woman. That's what they always told me to be. Don't depend on anyone and be very independent and that always stuck in my head. It got so bad to where that's just in me. I took it to another level of being independent and would not ask for anything. I would really be down and out but just stick it out.

THIS IS MY STORY, THIS IS MY SONG

POEM

I'M GROWING INTO THIS YOUNG LADY WITH SO MUCH RESPECT.

WITH THE LOVE OF GOD, A GREAT FAMILY SO MY LIFE SEEMED TO BE IN CHECK

NOT KNOWING HOW COLD THIS WORLD WOULD BE,

I'M LIVING THIS LIFE AND SOON I WOULD SEE.

I WAS BLESSED TO HAVE A PRAYING GRANDMOTHER,

WHO LOVED AND CARED FOR ME LIKE THERE WAS NO OTHER.

NOT KNOWING HER LATE NIGHT PRAYERS WAS OFTEN FOR ME,

SHE PLEADED THE BLOOD OF JESUS AND TOLD THOSE DEMONS TO FLEE

IN MY HEART I KNEW HER AND GOD WAS BEST FRIENDS,

HER SHOUTS, AND PRAISE WOULD WORK OUT IN THE END.

GRANDMA RAISED ME TO CALL ON GOD SO MUCH,

WHEN I GREW UP I WAS BLESSED WITH THESE HANDS THAT HAD HIS TOUCH.

THANK YOU GOD AND I LOVE YOU GRANDMA!

So I was happy with what I was doing. Working getting money and had a best friend with me that I loved just like my sister Temeka Harley but she now is married with kids and last named changed. We went through alot together and she is and always will be my best friend, my sister, my boo. We kept each other grounded and was always there for one another. I also had a group of 4 sisters I loved dearly and we did a lot of crazy, crazy, crazy things together but no matter what we was always there for one another. I did lose contact with them for many years and when I see them now my heart is always going back feeling like they were my babies, little sisters, and all I want is the best for them (you ladies know who you are…Tamara, Yolanda, LaKesha A. & LaKesha S.).

    Temeka and I are still in contact and she's always telling me to come out to visit her. We make plans to always see one another but it's pretty hard. I'm glad we have Facebook because we see one another growing and our families growing. Whenever something happen in my life I call her and we talk. We never had a fuss or anything. We were there for one another no matter what.

    So going back with me moving in with a family member. I always came back around the neighborhood but I only moved about 15 min away. So one day I was walking down the street just coming from my grandparents' home and some random guy stopped in the middle of the street and said hello. He was in his car, and I responded with a hello also. He then pulled over and I was nervous because I never saw him before but everyone was outside so I knew he couldn't do anything to me.

    So I looked up at my grandparents' house and I saw my grandmother looking at me. I was headed to a neighborhood around the corner from me to see my girlfriends. I felt safe so I talked to the guy for a bit and he seemed very nice. We exchanged numbers and instead of heading to my friends I just went back to my grandparents' house. As soon as I walked home my grandmother asked me who that young man. She told me to be careful. I was a scary type of person anyway.

I would always listen to grandma and my aunt Nadine because if they said don't go out tonight. Which me and my girlfriends would do often and the times when we decided not to (thinking about what my aunt and grandma would say) then we would hear of something bad happening in that area we were headed to. That's enough to make you nervous. So that guy called me often but I never answered. It was awhile before he actually heard my voice. From there we started talking a lot and I guess I was the type that gave people chances. He was one of them but I told a few people about him.

They knew him so that made it a little easier for me to give a chance to just be friends. I didn't want anything more than friends. I knew that having a boyfriend would lead to him wanted sex and I just didn't want it. So one day

I decided to meet up with him but it was by my home. Around the corner because I didn't want him to know where I was staying at the time.

So he would come over and we would talk in the parking lot on many of occasions. At this time I had just turned 19 and a virgin with no intentions on giving my body away. I felt great about me holding out and staying a virgin. I knew God was happy with me and my decision with not having sex. We have been talking for a few months and nothing ever been about sex. I never even laid up on him to make him feel any type of way sexual.

I felt very comfortable with him because he wasn't trying to get it from me and he was respecting me and my body. That made me trust him. One day he asked me to ride with him to his home quickly and he would bring me back. I then got a quick nervousness in my gut. He must have seen it in my face or something because he then stated that he is only picking something up for his friend to drop off to him. I said "sure that's fine"…why did I go? (I have no idea).

I took a quick peek at the place where I was staying at the time and said ok. I trust him! He wouldn't do anything bad to me because he's so nice and he don't talk about sex and a few people I know and trust knows him. That was my first time getting in the car with him. He told me that he had his own place. So we are driving and we get to his place. He said to me "come on in real quick".

My heart started pounding and I said "no I'll wait here in the car for you". He said "alright, I'll be right back. He went into his place and I was sitting there like what the heck I got myself into. He was taking a bit too long and now I was like let me just knock on the door and hurry him up. I watched him go into his apartment and the door he went into. I went up to the door and I knocked but stood back thinking he may just pull my little butt in the house.

Now I didn't tell you the size of this man to me. I'm 5"2 and weighed about 125 lbs. He was built with muscles weighing about 230 lbs (all muscle) which I was attracted to and about 6 ft. 3in or more (don't quote me on how tall) but he was way taller than me. I still gave him the benefit of the doubt that he was good people. I was a good person so nothing bad would happen to me. I knocked on the door and he answered and quickly apologized for the long wait.

The moment my life changed in his hands

He was getting some stuff together that he had to drop off to a friend. I said ok, and he said come in. I didn't want to be outside alone but didn't really want to go into the house. I told myself that I would just stand by the door and if he tried something I would run out the door and start screaming so someone would help me. So I walked in 2 steps and stood directly by the door. He walked into the kitchen where I could see him and ask did I want something to drink. I said "no thank you".

He then said "you can sit and relax on the couch, I'll be right back". So I said "no, I'm fine"! He headed into the back room and I then felt I wanted to throw up I was so nervous. I started to walk toward the couch so that I could try and peak around the corner into his room to see what he was really doing. I walked like about 2 steps from the door and he came out. He said "come here real quick". I was startled and froze up.

That was my queue to get the hell out of there and was so scared my mind was yelling run run run but my body just stood and wouldn't move. I was confused because I was so close to that door but I couldn't get to it. I was scared that he was going to beat me so bad and kill me. Everything was running through my head. I still couldn't move my feet to run. He took my wrist and started pulling me into his bedroom. I was saying "please, I don't want to go" I kept telling him to let me go but he kept saying it was alright.

I was thinking to myself I'm going to find something close and knock him in his head so I can get the heck out of there. Now because I had trust for someone that never talked about sex, was a gentleman he's not letting me leave when I'm begging him. He pulled me into his room and shut the door. He told me to be quite with a face that I said if I yell I won't make it out this house. He started pulling my clothes off and they came of really quick while I'm fighting to keep them on. He pulled everything off where I was naked and I knew this was the end of my virginity.

I didn't want to lose that until my husband was blessed with it. He pushed me on the bed and his body weight was too much for me and he laid on top of me. I was trying to hold my legs very tight but that didn't faze this guy and this time I am crying telling him no please let me leave and I promise I won't tell. At one time he said are you sure you won't. I swore I will not tell anyone and he didn't care. He opened my legs with the ease of one hand and his legs and that's when I felt his penis touching the outside of my vagina. I cried and kept begging for him to get off but he started to penetrate me and I yelled and screamed.

All I could do was think of why I got in the car with him. I was starting to blame everything on myself…but I tried to take my mind out of that room but the pain was unbearable. He kept telling me to be quiet but I couldn't. He was kissing my neck, and tried to kiss my lips but I kept moving my head back and forth and my face and his pillow was soak with my tears. I kept trying to pushing him off by his shoulders, I tried to tighten up my legs but nothing helped. I was in pain and didn't know what he did to me down there.

It felt like forever for him to stop but he did and got up off me and said that was good and I was wonderful. I was shaking so much I didn't know if I would be able to stand up thinking I may faint. He wouldn't leave my side but then quickly went into the bathroom and came right back. He pulled me to my feet and blood was all over me so now I know why he ran into the bathroom. To get something to wipe himself off. He walked towards me with a washcloth and tried to clean me off.

I jumped and didn't want him to touch me. He told me to wipe myself up but couldn't do much because of the pain. He got dressed and I did to but I kept my eye on him while he was just staring at me. I didn't think I was going to make it out that house but I got dressed and he said "are you ready to go home". I shook my head yes and he told me come on.

As I was trying to walk I was in so much pain, I looked back at the bed when I was barely walking out the bedroom and I saw blood on his sheets.

    I knew I would never forget this day if I was actually going to make it out alive. He walked in front of me and opened the door and I walked out. I was scared to put up a fuss I just wanted to get home and he was taking me there. In the car this dude said nothing the whole ride. We turned to my area and he let me off where he thought I lived. He said "I want to see you again"!

    I thought to myself, this guy is out of his mind. In my mind I was cussing him out fighting, hitting him and asking him why but I wanted to see familiar faces so I can know I am safe. I just had my head down and shook it yes, so I can get out of his car. I wasn't thinking about anything so I forgot he didn't know where I lived so started heading to my house.

I just kept telling myself...hurry and get in the house Dominique hurry and get in the house. I opened the door to my home and took off to my room.

My brothers was there and could tell something wasn't right. He said "what's wrong with you"? I said "nothing" and went into my room and locked the door. All of a sudden I didn't know my brothers went outside and I don't know what they told him because he had followed me home but I never saw or heard from him again. I cried in my room but tried to act like nothing happened.

I took my shower and went back into my room. I cried and cried and then moved back with my grandparents. They told me that I can always come back home and so I did. I never told anyone until one day a couple months after it happen I talked to one person and that person said to me "why did you go into the house"? I explained to this person how everything went down and that person said "well you shouldn't have went into the house".

    I then said to myself I will never tell anyone because it was my fault. I kept that promise to myself all of these years. It had me scared of men for a while but eventually I was introduced to a guy that was a friend of my girlfriend and he was really nice. I felt that sex was now a part of my life so why not give him a chance. I was so scared though but he talked to me, took his time with me and we had sex. He just didn't know that I tears was falling down my face but it was because I was remembering that day.

    I still kept it away and thought to myself my life would be changed because of what that man done to me. A year later I felt that I was alright but I was still afraid to have sex.

Trying to move on

That memory played over and over in my head and all I could do is just try to live with it. I tried hard to push it to the back of my mind and don't let anyone suspect something was going on with me so I hid it. I can tell you that the experience change alot of things in my head.

{I now know how girls that has been raped think differently about themselves. I've heard girls say that they feel like they are sluts or hoes because of what happened in their being raped. My mindset changed because I just didn't feel like myself anymore. He took something so precious from me that I can never get back and left me to deal with it. Girls become very sexually active but i'm not doctor that can say exactly why but my experience with it definitely changed me about the sexual part of my life}

I met a guy that at first I didn't want anything to do with just a friendship but he was really cool and I fell for the friend in him. Still cautious and my guard was always up being around a guy period. I made sure it was always my friends around. I never was alone with a guy for a very long time. I knew that I wanted a family still one day so I figured I find a great man that would protect me now and later eventually we will have a family. I kept the fact that me feeling like I was raped (I didn't know what to call it because I blamed myself) would be hard for me to try and have sex once again.

I now felt that I messed up something that I had special with God and I couldn't get that back. Now at this time my mind frame kind of switched and I wasn't so innocent and pure. This new friend of mind we hit it off. Now, I knew that I already basically had sex even though I was forced so if this guy wanted to have sex and I liked him it wouldn't or shouldn't be a problem or matter for me. This would be my 2nd encounter with sex. That's what I was telling my mind.

I really felt a connection with this guy and started falling for him as well as he was falling for me. The first time that we had sex was very difficult for me. He wanted to get right to intercourse and not take his time with foreplay my body would shut down and think it's going through that horrible rape and at the end of having sex then I would be so sore. I dealt with it hoping that this part of my life would get better in time and of course hoping sooner than later. So, this guy and I had a good time and enjoyed each other's company. He loved having me around and vice versa.

The sex part for me was painful because no matter what my body always would shut down (meaning I wouldn't get aroused). By him still pushing himself into me would make me tense up even more. It always ended up with me sore or ripped but I didn't want to tell him what I went through because I thought this was all my fault. I use to go and stay with him over the weekends and come back home to my grandparents. One day after I came back from his house I received a call from him. He said "I just want to tell you something"! I was waiting and said "ok, what is it".

    He said "You're pregnant"! I laughed out loud and said "no I am not". He said "yes you are! Go get checked and call me to tell me what the doctor says". That was the funniest thing ever. I didn't know that he had a good reason to know. He told me later on that he planned to get me pregnant. We always used a condom but he admitted to taking it off and I was so naive I didn't know much about sex hands on.

    He said it was something about me and I was different than any other girl and he wanted me to be his child's mother. So, I called my girls up and we talked about it. I said to myself, let me just go to the doctors and prove to this fool I'm not pregnant. He was waiting for that call and I called and gave him the news "I am pregnant". He was so happy! He was absolutely excited and couldn't wait to see his child. I always wanted my career in servicing celebrities, a husband & a child in that order.

    I just wanted to be happy and didn't need to be rich. Just living comfortable with my family is all I ever wanted. Even though his excitement was there for his child and having me as his wife (that's what he said) his behavior for the mother of his child was beginning to be obnoxious and disgusting. I thought since he had a great woman on his side that would do anything in the world for him, he would see that and feel it in his heart to be a great man and father. When I use to come down and spend time with him without my girls he was a great guy, we chilled in together all day. Drove out sometimes but mostly in the house with his family whom he tried to get me to get really close to.

I was so shy so I was afraid to go around them. I would stay in his room all day long if I could. Lol yes that sounds so weird but that's how shy I was. Whenever I actually sat down with them I was very quiet. The family was an awesome loving family. I had so much love for them and they had no clue at the time.

I knew being a part of the family would be something I would love knowing the love they had to share. I was pregnant the same time his older sister was pregnant. She had her son six months before I had my son Oldest. She was a very beautiful woman inside and out. She always asked her brother do I need anything or she would tell him to let me know I can come and talk with her if I wanted to. I wanted to go and talk with her and their little sister but I was nervous.

I wish I had because not long after I actually met her and was coming around she passed away. A very beautiful person and I never got the chance to spend time with her I spent most of the time with him. When I was pregnant I didn't know they knew and like I said I was nervous and shy I stayed to myself. The few times that I did come upstairs and sit in the living room it was because I was going through it with my boyfriend. When I was a few months pregnant he kind of started drinking and it turned him into it seemed like another person.

    He would argue with me for no reason but I would just sit there and pray that he would stop and he would end up falling asleep. It then started getting better because he said that he felt that when he did drink alcohol he would feel different. I would tell him what he would say to me and how he would argue with everyone. He stopped for a while. Then one day after work I came down and he just got off from work he was pretty intoxicated. My ride had dropped me off already and I didn't think that anything bad would go down.

First signs of abuse are there just listen to your heart

This was my very first situation of abuse in this form. I didn't think that I had to worry about a man fighting me for any reason because I'm such a kind hearted person. The first day that he put his hands on me was a huge shock to me. I was just sitting very quiet watching television in his room (He had the whole basement to himself). I was pretty big at this time maybe around 7 months pregnant. He was outside with a few of his friends. He had a back door that he used to go in and out of.

He came in and was drunk. I just looked at him really to see how drunk he was. He started saying some evil things and I just was tired of it and yelled back at him. He took his hand and backhanded me across my face. He knocked my jaw out of socket because I couldn't close my mouth all the way. It hurt to try and close my mouth.

The first thing I saw close to me was a telephone. I grabbed it quickly before he could hit me again and I swung it across his face as hard as I could. It hit him in his ear and he started screaming because it hurt, he got an instant ringing in his ear and he couldn't hear for a minute (That's what he told me). He grabbed me, pushed me on his bed and just started chocking me. Now at this time mind you I'm pregnant with his child but alcohol isn't a joke. He choked me and all I could do was smack, hit until I starting seeing nothing but darkness.

I was passing out and he didn't know until I stopped fighting back. All I remember was feeling a nudge like I was being hit, shaken, but all I know it didn't hurt. I had passed out! The next thing I could remember is when I open my eyes and see without it being blurry he was holding me very close and tight to his chest telling me to breath. God was there for both of us. He apologized and promised that he would never put his hands on me ever again.

I told him the next time (me and giving chances) I would leave and he would never see me or his child again in life. When I came to while he was holding me I was confused and didn't know what happen. So, staying there with him through this was like me not ignoring that he just most likely killed me and his son. God brought me back. I just was feeling really confused about the situation. Another episode is after I had my son. We was downstairs and he was fighting me and it's sad to say but it was the normal until he grabbed my son up and said "he's my son and I'm not going to hurt him".

He was so drunk and barley could walk

alone. I didn't think that he was going to intentually hurt him. I just thought that since my boyfriend was that drunk that he would fall down the steps or something and drop my baby. When I would say something to my boyfriend he would snap on me but he never hit me in front of his family. I had to just go sit upstairs with his parents and say nothing until he calmed down. One day sitting outside with his friend and myself just having a normal conversation but me not saying much just sitting there.

    He all of a sudden just started pouring liquor on top of my head, through my weave that was cute and it just ran down my face. His friend said to him "Man why the hell would you do that to her? She didn't do anything to you. She's a really good person and you need to stop. Stop disrespecting her like that". That pissed him off because he thought that his friend was taking up for me and told me to leave with him. I got up to hit him and he knocked my little butt down.

That wouldn't stop me from coming after him but he ended up dragging me around the back of the house where he would take me into his room and the fighting would continue. He swung at his friend and I told the guy just leave and I would be alright. I didn't want them to fight. It was this liquor that had control over him. I told his friend just leave and I will be fine. I went to his father and he would talk to me and tell me to not let him disrespect me.

I felt safe when I did sit around his mom and dad. I love them so much and their spirits are just as peaceful and loving. No matter what I was going through with my boyfriend at the time I never let them know what was going on and they would be right in the house. I was that quiet and was just hoping things would get better. I believe it was only twice that they knew something was going on bad and they told me to come in with them and I called a family member to come and get me. In the beginning it was fun and nice being around but then it got to the point I thought I wasn't going to live and I did nothing wrong.

    Only tried to love him but he was a drinker and every time he would drink with his friends something bad would happen. I tried to get him to stop because if he wouldn't drink he was the sweetest person and we would hold great conversations, we would go places and just enjoy one another. Making plans for our future was the best because we both had goals that was realistic and we could achieve. As soon as that liquor came into play it was the smart remarks, hitting, choking you name it I went through it. I decided that I couldn't help him no matter how much I tried so the day he finally took me home I said nothing the whole ride home. I'm sure he knew something was wrong but I played it off like I was cool.

All I was thinking about was let me see my house I'm getting the hell out and I'm telling him right away that I am done. We finally reached my home and I got out and got my son with our belongings. He said to me "You aren't coming to see me anymore are you?" Outside of the car with my son and our things I looked at him and said "You're right"! I told him I can't do this any longer. I just started walking to my door and when I opened that door I knew my son and I was safe. I laid up on my grandmother and just said nothing.

The phone rang not long after I walked in the house. Someone yelled "Nique, the phone is for you!" My grandmother said "tell them to call back". She knew something was wrong and wanted me to just take some time and get back to being me. My son was just the happiest baby ever and all he did was smile and laugh with his big cheeks. He kept me in a good place when I felt sad but he kept me alive.

I decided to talk to my grandmother and tell her what I was going through. She was my best friend but I choose what to tell her because I didn't want to hurt her knowing what I was going through. I talked to her about the abuse with my boyfriend (not all the abuse). The day I came home I couldn't eat and I was so hungry. That was the first thing my grandmother offered me when I was home. I couldn't eat because the night before when my boyfriend at the time was on his rage.

He hit me so hard in my face it did something to my jaw once again but this was worst. I couldn't close my mouth all the way. Whenever I tried to it hurt so bad so I had to tell my grandmother. So while we were upstairs in my room getting me back settled in I was telling her I want to eat but it hurts so try to close my mouth all the way. Mind you I dealt with this for many hours so she walked out my room for a second and came back. I started to talk to her and I heard and felt this click in my mouth.

It felt like my jaw was knocked out of its socket but as quickly as I heard and felt the click. My jaw just fell back into place and I started to close my mouth with no problem. I never thought right away that my grandmother and her prayer did that. I was just so happy that I could close my mouth all the way. Man, home I swear never felt so good like always. I got the phone call again and I answered it. Who do you think was on the other end of the line?

If you said my sons father than you are right. The famous line "I'm sorry! I will never hurt you again!" Yes, those lines from an abusive man so when I woman go back it's just a reoccurring act of abuse and I didn't enjoy this man telling me that he loved me and I am special but you would hit me, disrespect me in any way possible. That's not love!!! I thought love was happiness, showing respect, helping, loving. I know what love is and it never hurt me or made me cry from pain.

It was the total opposite. He put me in a place of when I felt anger or upset in any way from someone my first reaction was to strike before they get me. I didn't like that feeling. I would jump when someone would just raise their hand, or loud noise and let an argument start up I would be there and would jump to the other person defense. I just hate when someone is being disrespected so I feel like I need to defend them. So that day on the phone I told him it was over and I meant it.

Soon after me getting home I took him to court because he kept saying I can't keep him from his son, he knew the places I would be, it was like he was stalking me. He said he had eyes on me at all times. I didn't tell my grandparents this because it would be like old times for them seeing a child of theirs going through abuse. My grandparents not knowing what happened with us invited him into the home to see his child. I couldn't deal with this anymore so I had a court date coming up from his abuse and I didn't try to keep him from his child but I didn't want him around me. I felt that if he came to my home to see our son I would be unavailable but close enough just in case. He didn't want that.

    He wanted me there also. My grandparents being the loving people they were still had love for him but they were making sure that we were safe first. He declined that so we took it to court and all I wanted was for him to stay away from me and be the great dad to our son I know he would be. I told the judge that my grandparents welcomed him in the home so that he can see his son but he declined. We even offered for him to meet a third party so that he can see his child but not at this time he couldn't take him away alone. I specifically told the judge I didn't want anything from him.

I could take care of my son on my own. So the judge said "I'm giving Ms. Jones full custody of the child and I issue the other party Mr.___ to pay child support. I didn't ask for money! I didn't want anything from him. When we walked out the courtroom and towards the car he had the nerve to tell me if I don't take him off of child support he will not have anything to do with my son. I told him "first of all I didn't put you on child support 2nd you have a great job making 10x what the judge issued you to pay. That wasn't anything to you so I told him to do what he wanted to.

So he choose to stay out of my son life and the tiny respect I had for him just being the father of my son was absolutely gone forever. The one thing I always wanted was for my son to have a father no matter what. I believe that's why I stayed in that abusive relationship as long as I did. It just wasn't worth it. I felt like this. I'm a strong woman and I know how I would want to be treated as a woman so I can only raise him to be a respectful, loving, caring, god fearing man the best I could.

I didn't have my biological mother or father in my life and I know how I felt that emptiness inside even though I had awesome grandparents in my life and took that roll. I felt they are my parents but still inside I had a void that couldn't be filled and I know how I would feel upset at times and really wasn't sure why. I just had lots of pain that was kept inside and didn't know how to really share. So it was me and my son for 5 yrs. together. No sex for me for 5 years and I didn't miss it because it was horrible how at times I had to do it to keep him from being angry and fight me. I didn't want a man because all I could think of is men have done the worst to me and I didn't want to feel that pain in anyway at all.

Moving on with my little blessing {My son}

So my son and I was best friends since he was born. He was my little buddy and he just don't know how he changed and saved my life. I was smoking weed with my dude before I found out I was pregnant. It was what I was around and it started not getting me high anymore. As soon as I felt that feeling of this isn't enough I found out I was pregnant with my oldest. He saved my life because that was the last time weed was a part of my life.

I thank God for blessing me with my son (he saved me). I tried to be the perfect little church girl that everyone thought Dominique was. I tried certain things to keep my mind of off the bad things that I had went through. I was a teen and I smoked weed, I tried drinking but didn't like that much (still drank though) being apart of the crowd it loosened me up. I smoked weed after I went through the rape and it just took my mind off of it so I did it often. I was a very depressed woman and looking into my little son eyes and his smiles was a way to take my mind off of my pain and look into his pure soul with no worries in the world.

He was now my world and I had to do what I had to make sure that he was safe. I didn't even talk to anyone because I was afraid that I would come across a guy that would just do me harm. My baby and I was just one. My grandparents often told me that I never had to leave or move out of the house and this was always our home. I knew that if I didn't become independent which they taught me then I would always need them. Even though I never wanted leave or to think about it I knew that one day they wouldn't be here on this earth.

They would be in heaven with God. Oh I hated to think about that cause I couldn't imagine life without them. Before I started looking into finding a place for me and my son I would often sit back and remember all the memories that I had at home.

MEMORIES

I remember when we first moved into the house at the end on pioneer Drive. We didn't rent a truck or anything because we lived so close we walked most of our things down the street. That was fun to me. With the big things was taken down by family in a car or whatever but I really don't remember too much of the move but I do know how much fun it was going into another home with my family and leaving bad memories there.

I remember my son always crawling into my grandparent's room, getting to the door and watching them. I would watch him the whole time to see what he would do. As soon as they would spot him they would say "Hey man, what are you doing and he would get happy and crawl real fast towards them and someone would pick him up. Granddad would say "Nique, you have to watch out for him because he's getting around now and he may try to go down the stairs".

I remember also one time my Grandfather was watching Jerry Springer…oh my goodness so I came in the room to see what granddad and Daeshaun was doing. They both was just sitting on the bed watching television. So I sat down playing with Daeshaun and he was more into the television. So I started watching it with them. All of a sudden on the television someone said "you b!@@h"…in my head I was like oh my goodness I hope he didn't hear that. A few minutes later everything was quiet and he says very quietly…"granddad, her a b!@@h". Granddad bust out laughing and said we have to watch what we let him see because he's always paying attention. We told him that was a bad word and we can't say that. He said "bad word, can't say that" and the next thing we knew he fell asleep under my grandparents pillows at the top of the bed. You could only see his foot and his hand sticking out the pillows.

My granddad laughed at what Daeshaun said for a while and had told grandma.

My grandparents still had this candy truck in the community and I was the one most of the time taking them to the store to stock up. I loved when my grandparents needed to go to the store. I think I was the only one that had lots of patience. Granddad would go down every single aisle and take forever but I didn't mind. The ride there and home was so fun. When Granddad, Grandma, Daeshaun and I rode out together it was really fun and lots of laughs about everything. Granddad had lots of jokes and both of my grandparents had stories about their past and family for days. I would sit in the room and listen to their stories. They loved whenever I came in the room just to sit. I just loved their company and I know they loved mine.

I remember when my little cousins teen teen

and Dave would come in my room looking for Daeshaun. I would let them in and they would play as long as they wanted. I would pick both of them up and put them in the crib with Daeshaun and all three was just laughing and having fun. I loved watching them play together. Grandma and Granddad would say that they will be close and growing up yes, they always had a bond that I always wanted them to keep. Teen Teen no matter what would always come around and show love. She is just the most loving person in the world and so humble. She's for family and what's right. Dave also has the most beautiful heart and loving person. Always wanting to help and them both stayed looking out for my son Daeshaun. They just don't know how much love I always will have for them and always would. They're my babies I don't care how old they will get they will always be my babies.

I remember when I found out that I was pregnant and I was so scared to tell my grandparents. In my head I had the most perfect conversation with them and telling them the news. Yea, that was in my head. One day I said let me tell my grandmother first. So I said to my grandmother while we were in the house alone. Granddad was on the candy truck. I started to say grandma I have to talk to you about something. She looked at me and said "Nique, how are you feeling?" I said "I'm fine but I want to talk to you about something. She looked at me again and said with a beautiful smile on her face "How are you and the baby doing?" My mouth just dropped and she said "dad and I already knew" all I could do was feel relief but also feel confused as why didn't they tell me when they knew. Grandma said "daddy knew first that's why he always asked me to keep check on you and make sure you take care of yourself and get checked by the doctor. So I didn't have to tell them they just knew and just knowing how much they were there for me then and now all I could do was be happy and blessed to have them as my parents. I knew that I would love my child the way my grandparents have always loved me but I felt that my child needs to meet such wonderful and loving grandparents so I was so happy that they would be a part of my child's life.

I had great memories in that home and never wanted to forget them.

Growing into my Independence

It was a lot of learning and growing so now it was my time to get my independence and move out with me and my little one. So that day came and I got my first place and I was about 22yrs old. Very spoiled with my grandparents still telling me that I don't have to move out but if I want to that's fine I will still have a home to come back to. The day came that my son Daeshaun and I moved into our very first place. He didn't understand that we wouldn't see grandma and granddad often as we had but now it would be him and I. That day Daeshaun got his first toddler bed with basketball bedding and I remember this because he loved basketball.

I brought him a little court so we could play in the house and he had a few basketballs around the house. This little boy was so spoiled and I loved him, kissed him on his fat face all the time and made sure I told him I loved him always and every single day. Those words was a couple words I taught him from the beginning of his life. I would say to him always "I lovvveeee yooouuuuu! Mommy! Thank you! I also use to sing this one song to him always and incorporate his name in it. "Oh how I love Jesus, Oh how I love Jesus, Oh how I love Jesus because he first loved me…Ohhhh

Daeshaun do you love Jesus?" I would answer for him until he was old enough to speak himself. "Oh yes I love Jesus!" "Are you sure you love Jesus?" "I'm sure I love Jesus!" "And why do you love Jesus?" "Because he first loved me, that's the reason we all should love him".

    I sang that song to all kids and any babies that I came around and held close to me. We had a great time moving in but the first night away from home was so different. I kept our schedule, well the schedule my grandparents had him on. I was a great mom but I let my grandparents raise him with me. I knew I wanted him to feel the love that they showed me all my life so he would have 2 other great family in his life. So my son and I had a great experience living alone. I'm growing into the great independent woman I was raised to be.

    My little man is growing and just happy as ever and we saw our grandparents as often as possible. I was working and he was being cared for by family. He loved his mommy and that's all that mattered to me. Everything seemed to be going well. I felt safe and I had my baby with me. We had lots of fun together and he was so spoiled. It didn't matter because he filled my life with more joy than he will ever know. I had been living in my new place for almost a year and at this time the rental office was doing construction on the apartments. I was going to work in the morning and getting home in the evening with my son. I always walked by the construction crew and spoke and kept it moving. I was one that never changed and had lots of respect but still so shy.

One day I came home and I felt very weird feeling inside my heart. I just felt like I wasn't alone and slowly I walked around my place. My son wasn't home at this time but I went into my room and I had a huge walk in closet. I knew that I had to open that door because I couldn't have my son coming into a dangerous situation. So I opened the closet and I saw these shoes that were mine but I know how I place anything in my home. They were moved just slightly and that startled me.

    Instantly my heart is pounding like somebody has been in my home and could still be here. I pulled out this little bat that I had named Ray Ray and I was hoping that I didn't have to use it. I slowly bent down to look under my bed and nothing. So the entire place was checked and no one was there but I still felt like someone was watching me. I checked all around my house looking at things and I could tell that so many things was touched and tried to be placed back the way I had them. Someone like me that's very keen on her things and know the way that I left something was going to find out.

    I don't know why I looked into my refrigerator but my food was moved also in the freezer was touched but nothing was missing. That just didn't make sense to me. Why not take our food instead of touching it and only try to scare a single woman with a very young child. Whomever did come into our home and did this had some intentions and I wasn't going to stay around to find out why. I had that feeling and I knew God was with me so I shouldn't be afraid but I wasn't going to be stupid and not say anything.

So I notified the management and you know they ask me was it something I am imagining. I asked them "Are you guys really stupid or dumb as hell?" How could you not right away go check out what was going on, and mind you the crew was still working but someone had a way to get into my home which had a top bolt lock where only you can access it with a key. They knew something wasn't right but I wasn't going to stay another night in that place. When my son was brought home to me right away I had almost everything packed up and ready to leave.

    I had contacted my Aunt Rita that was a rental agent and right away she said give me about a week and I will have you ready and in your own place. About an hour after talking to my Aunt and my grandparents everyone was there packing up our things. My son and I moved back in with my grandparents until our place was ready. We was closer to all of the family and I loved that. I don't know what ever happen with the rental office because my least wasn't up just yet. I told them I was leaving that day and I wasn't taking anything from them.

    My son and I was with my grandparents for about a week and they loved having us back home but I knew I had to keep going with having my own home. I have been spoiled all my life and I knew I had to raise my son to be very independent. I was so spoiled that my

Aunts would come to my home out the blue and clean my home top to bottom. Everyone always called me spoiled rotten, fur coat (Aunt Nadine) lol, she already ate was an inside joke with my Aunt Nadine and Uncle (me being nosey when I was a child). My Aunt Rita was the lifesaver that helped me into my home in the back of Richfield and I had to pay rent every month like everyone else. I appreciated her for helping me and my son when I was in that crazy situation.

That's what family is for helping one another and being there for each other. It doesn't have to be money related. It could be listening and I was always be one of many that you could just come to and talk, vent, cry or whatever and I would take it in and pray about it. The day, the move for me and my son came was a great move. I was excited to decorate my son room that he had to himself. He was excited also so we move in and I thanked God for allowing this all to happen but didn't go through my home with prayer right away.

    I wasn't sure why my son kept coming in my room saying something was in his room and he didn't want to sleep in his room. We would walk back in the room so I can check it out and I would tell him to pray and lay down but I didn't at the time take him back to his room. I would only pray with him and let him get in the bed with me. That made him feel safe and that's all I knew since I was doing the same to stay close to my grandparents. So one night when he went to bed in his room he woke up out the blue screaming bees are all in my room. He would say a man was in the room and of course that would scare the heck out of me.

    I would check it out but never once saw anyone. I myself after dealing with my home invasion at our very first home couldn't sleep much. I constantly walked my home up and down the stairs checking to see if my windows was locked, my doors was locked, making sure that anything in my home wasn't out of place. This was something I did ever since my first home. I had to make sure my son was safe and nothing ever happen to him. I would put chairs up at the door so if someone tried to get in I would have enough time to call for help.

So that night my son came into my room with me saying that he had lots of bees in his room, I got out of bed, checked his room out and we sat on the side of his bed and I said a prayer with him. I said it and he copied me word from word. I tell you that night he got in the bed and I tucked him in, said goodnight and gave him mommy kisses he fell right to sleep. Every night since then he would not have a problem sleeping in his room. Sometimes I would tell him to come in the room with me and watch television. He would say I'm sleepy and get up to go to his room and I would say "sleep in the room with mommy".

He would say "No, I want to sleep in my bed". I couldn't do anything but laugh at this little man that I didn't want to grow up on me. I remember giving him kisses all the time but around the age of 5 he became a man and wasn't supposed to kiss girls including me. I loved having my little man all to myself but at the same time I hated that he was growing up without a father. I would hear from his father every now and then but not so much would my son. When his father did call and I would give Daeshaun the phone he didn't know how to talk to Daeshaun.

He would talk to him as he was a baby and Daeshaun would give the phone to me with this crazy look on his face like (what is he talking about). You know even though his father wasn't in his life and he didn't talk to him often at all like maybe twice in a year. I still talked good about his dad in front of him and made sure he had respect for his dad. I had a few pictures of his dad and he knew what he looked like. I would ask him do he love his dad and he would tell me yes. I knew I did a good job and my little man heart was of gold.

He is the type that loved everyone but as he got older his feelings he didn't show as much but little things he would do or say you definitely could tell he had your back and he loved you. My son and I lived a fun life because I had him to hang with, spoil and we stayed around grandma, granddad and the family. We lived walking distance from them so if they needed us or we just wanted to be around them we could. I wasn't worried about a man and I wasn't thinking about any. I thought it would be my son and myself for ever and I was absolutely fine with that. We was living in this townhome for a few years and everything was going well.

I was working, coming home to my son

and that's about it. We would spend time together at parks, out to eat, church (we loved going to church). One night my son wanted to stay at my grandparents' home. My cousin Sheneea who lived about 6 doors down from us was having a fight party at her and her husband house with a few of his friends, family. I came down to see her quickly but I wasn't planning on staying long. I came in and spoke to everyone.

Everyone was walking back and forth through the house. I loved seeing my cousins we would sit and talk and laugh. It was two of my cousins Carlet and Sheneea that lived in this area with me. Just doors away from one another and our Aunt Evon was doors away from us also. My cousin told me that her husband was going to talk to me about his friend that was interested in me. I looked at her and was like ohhhhh no because I just didn't know how to talk to a guy.

It's been so long and I didn't have any interest but I didn't want anyone to think I was being stuck up or disrespectful if I said I wasn't interested. I couldn't do it! I was so nervous because I just wasn't ready. I just thought I wasn't ready but it have been 5 years that I've been out of this abusive relationship and I had to tell myself that I had to get over it. My family knew what I was going threw just not everything. I had to think about it and feel that all men wasn't bad out here. Still I am a good woman so who wouldn't want to make me a happy woman and be a great role model for my son. Whoever, would be blessed to find me and be in our lives. In the middle of my cousin telling me who it was and me not knowing because I wasn't paying anyone any attention. He decided to walk by again and she had to say "this is like the third time he walked by". I was like dag he must be really interested. We laughed because I didn't see him either of those times and I was nervous to look up and seem to be all in his face.

He then stopped and ask me can he talk to me for a minute out front. I agreed and we talked and it was a nice conversation. Actually it was a very long conversation that both really enjoyed. He asked for my number and said he wanted to talk sometimes. I gave him my number and we talked on the phone a lot. Everyday this guy was saying "Good morning, he's thinking of me," He was a nice guy from what I gathered and nice looking also.

I just wasn't sure where I wanted to go with this but he was really interested in me. He was taking it a little faster than what I wanted but I felt it as a good guy, no kids, no girlfriend and not living around the way (All a plus). We just talked for a few months and went out often spending time with my son and myself was a great feeling. My son fell in love with him and they played games and he would take him to get his hair cut. He really was taking my heart where I prayed that I wanted it to go. I said after talking and meeting his parents that he was serious and I went with the flow. My son liked him and that made me more interested in him.

That really played a big part a man being in my life only if my son liked him and how he took to my son. His parents met my son and his father really took to my son. My son fell in love with his father because he wanted to go with them all of the time and he use to tell me that he love him. I was shocked and was hoping this would be what I deserved. When I met them he brought me to the house.

I was a little nervous to go in and meet them but I didn't want them to look at me as I was being disrespectful. So we walked in the house and they met me at the door. He introduced me to them and I felt great vibes from them. Everything was going really good with me and this new guy in my life. I could tell he was a good guy but the company that he was keeping wasn't good really. I felt like this.

If you are telling your friends that you are taking your lady out to spend time with her and your friend talks negative about you showing them up because they weren't doing it with their lady. I don't know why but he felt some type of commitment to these dudes that just wanted to see him fail. I saw it but still I rode with him thinking that things would be good and we would grow together. I wasn't expecting to have a great relationship but near it, yes. We spent a lot of time together him, Daeshaun and myself with his family also.

I felt really comfortable with them and I love how his family was very close and did everything together. Our relationship was growing and we were falling in love. It was one problem…that one so called friend. I was saying more than I should and telling him to stand up for himself or I would take control which

I didn't mind. I had a lot of fight in me since it seemed that I had to do this a lot before this relationship. I totally carried my past relationship along with me.

He was the first man I love and gave my time to since my abusive relationship. My current boyfriend would tell me things that this friend use to tell him. Like he would tell my boyfriend that he needs to stop spending all this time with me, he would intervene when he knew my boyfriend would say we are doing something and he would ask for a ride or something stupid. In the middle of this that I thought I could handle because it wasn't physical between us I thought this would be easy to fix. Not quit!

Within that year I found out that I was pregnant. I was happy, Daeshaun was happy and so was my boyfriend. He was so excited to tell his parents. He was talking marriage and I didn't reject. All I asked was for him to respect me and my son and now our child I was carrying. He promised and we just started living our life.

His mom and I was talking a little about the wedding and my dress. The funny part about that was his mom asked me what color dress was I going to wear. I told her white and she said "oh no, you can't wear white"! See I knew that I wasn't supposed to wear white because I already had sex before marriage. I just knew that I wouldn't look good in that color off white. No I couldn't think what would go with it but that was a funny discussion my boyfriend and I was having.

We were happy about this new bundle of joy coming into the world and at this time I'm still working, taking care of my son and my home. That's just what I had to do. I'm getting bigger and bigger with the baby and it starts. The late nights, the text in the phone (and yes I looked), I have to run him here quickly but turned into lies. I was having his first child and why would I have to be put on the back burner for anyone but God and in some situations your family. He knew how big I was on family and keeping it together. So what do you think I did when all of this was going on? Did I stay or did I go?

Well, if you said "I stayed" you are right (that thing called love and giving a chance). All I ever want for my son and myself was a man that loved us with everything in him and God was his first priority. This man here definitely grew up knowing God so I thought things would be different with him. He tried to prove to me that he wanted me and everyone could tell that the love for me he had was incredible. One day my boyfriend and I had a cookout and all the family and friends came through. I was shocked at the outcome but my Grandmother, so many of my cousins and my Aunts came.

I remember standing at the front door and for some reason I looked back into the kitchen and my boyfriend and my eyes just connected. We stood there looking at each other and I felt that love so deep and that's how he was looking at me. We ended up smiling at one another and I winked at him and we continued to greet everyone while he was cooking on the grill. We was in love and things started getting much better. Well the time got very close to me to deliver our baby girl and it was also a very scary situation. One day I didn't feel the baby move for that whole entire day.

  I thought just because she was big and didn't have really any room to move around. My doctor was saying that she's going to be a huge baby and that made me so nervous. I wasn't sure if she would be able to come out vaginally or not. Yes they had me so nervous. So I had a doctor's visit that day I still didn't feel her moving around. I was at work this day also but my supervisor let me go in for my appointment and come back to work.

I go in and the visit goes quickly because I thought they were going to check her heart beat and all but they were discussing what was ready to happen when it was time. So they started to make the last appointment. I stopped and said "You didn't listen for her heart beat and I haven't felt her move for a whole day". They said "ok, let's check her out". They took me inside the examining room and started to listen for her heart rate. Couldn't find one.

They did all kind of things to wake her up. They put an electric pencil sharpener on my stomach and started it with a pencil to see if she would wake up. Nothing, so they checked other things and right away told me to go directly to the hospital because she had to be born right away. She was in distress and they put me in to have an emergency caesarean. They told me not to stop for anything. I was to go directly to the hospital.

Do you know how scared they had me? I was told not to even to go get her dad. I had to call him on the phone and tell him to meet me. My doctor's office was down the street from my job so I called my cousin that was working Carlet (I love you so much) and since we was related to the manager she was able to leave with me. I did a quick 2 sec drive by a she jumped in with me and we were on the way to the hospital. We get there and they start prepping me right away.

My cousin Tierra came through and my Uncle James. My boyfriend got there in time before I walked to the operating room. We walked to my surgery together and this was going to be the last day that we would be a family of 3 it would be a family of 4 if everything went well. We would have a boy and a girl. So I remember laying down and they are hooking me up to everything. I'm hearing beeping noises, nurses talking and the doctor getting ready and then I fall off to sleep. The next thing I remember is waking up in the recovery room laying in a bed all alone and I turn to see my love sitting beside me with a baby wrapped up in a blanket (our daughter).

He asked me am I alright and now I'm concerned because I didn't see this baby moving in the blanket she was wrapped in. I just couldn't wait to see this big baby I was scared to have virginally. As I'm waking up slowly and anxious I looked at him and said "let me see her". He pulled back the cover off of the baby. I see this tiny little baby that looked nothing like me (her dad was all over her) but she was laying there so peaceful and sleep. Thank you God for blessing us with our daughter. I'm just coming off my meds that had put me to sleep.

Then I think about what my doctor was telling me about her size and I'm a little concerned now. I told him that baby wasn't mine. He had a slight laugh and said "yes, this is your baby". I asked him was he there the entire time they took her out of my stomach. He said "yes, I never left her side". My daughter was supposed to be about 8lbs-9lbs and she came out 4lbs. She looked nothing like me at all. She looked just like her dad.

    She was very tiny but was completely healthy where she came in the room with me right away. My 5 year old son Daeshaun came to see his little sister and was happy to meet her and hold her (she fit perfectly into his arms). He couldn't wait until she came home. She was so tiny that my doctor and nurses called her little peanut. It was hard to explain why she was in distress and so tiny. She was in perfect health coming into this world is what they told me. So I was put into my room and she was able to come in with me. Yes, she was 4lbs but she had no problems at all just very tiny.

Her big brother came in and was happy so we had family to come in and visit. My baby began to be very fussy and we had no clue why. She was fed and changed so we knew something was wrong. Before the visitors she was a much quit baby, just made little noises when she was ready to eat but I had to wake her to get her to eat most of the time. So family started visiting and she began to become more and more fussy. I had to call the nurse in so they can check on her.

I remember the nurse coming in and telling us that they know why she's fussy. They were reading her chart and said her arm was broken. For the life of me I couldn't figure out how my 4lb baby arm was broken when she was taken out by caesarian. Every time we touched her arm or moved her much she would cry. The doctor came in and was confused because he would've put this in our file about her arm. They told us to keep her wrapped up in the blanket with her arm tight to her body until they came back in the room.

At this time my baby became fussier and I was extremely upset. My daughter's grandmother begun to get upset also and said she was going to get a lawyer (oh yeah we were on it). A few minutes later the doctor and nurses came in and wanted to give me and our family on apology. I was really confused at this time. They had another "Jones" on the floor and they had our charts mixed up. My daughter was perfectly fine and as soon as they said it was a mix up with the charts I removed the blankets from her.

I lift her arm, moved it all around and not one cry. My daughter just didn't like a lot of people around and noise. She just wanted to be in her mom arms with peace and quiet. It's funny because that's how she is till this day. She is 14 now but always played by herself and a very quiet little girl. She stays in her room or a quiet place reading a book or something like that.

So, when I was moving her arms around and she didn't make a noise everyone even the doctor and nurse looked at each other and was like (this little baby tricking us).

The day went by great and we was blessed that our baby girl Amanie was just fine. In the hospital they would do hearing test on all babies. They did the test on my peanut a few times in the time that we were there and she kept failing it. They told me that since she didn't come through the birth canal she may still have a little fluid in her ear and they will retest her a little later in the doctor's office. We came home with her and I had family there to help me out since I had a C-section. I couldn't wait to see my son (Daeshaun) and for him to bond with his sister.

When we got home he was waiting at the

door for us. I unwrapped her out of the blankets and I sat on the couch so my son can hold his sister. He sat beside me and I put her in his arms (he loved holding her. I was in pain so I went to rest and my cousin Lisa stayed with me for a while to help me out. I wasn't getting much rest because I would here in my ear "you aren't bleeding down there so we can have sex". That was my boyfriend (ha-ha). He knew I didn't want to but like always I gave in to keep him happy…I know.

It was a couple of days that he just kept asking so yes I gave in. I wasn't thinking clearly and was so upset that he kept bugging me about making love to him. Yes, I just had a C-section but I did give in. I was so in a hurry to get it over because I needed my rest. I just didn't care so guess what (no condom). I thought about it in the middle of it I remembered but yes too late.

He was happy and I knew I needed to

keep my man that way. I did what I had to do (shoulder shrugs). So while taking care of a home, 2 kids and juggle a job it was alright. Soon after I was able to heal from my C-Section I was on the roll with my kids with work, church and spending time with them. I would spend most of my time with my son but my boyfriend's parents stepped up and always involved my son in their family. His parents would pick my daughter up every other weekend.

My son bonded with them but really bonded with my man's father. Having that man in his life that he no longer had was great and it felt like it was on the right track and it was a plus because they loved God and walked in his footsteps.

So back to my story.

I'm taking care of business and a couple of months go by and I'm putting on some weight. At work my co-workers and I would get together and have bets. Like when we thought we gained weight we would see who would lose the most weight in a period of time. This was one of those times. It seemed like we all would put on weight together. So we did and I did gain weight with my little peanut.

    I was doing great and I lost a lot in a month. If you ever heard that when you lose a lot of weight that is what happens when you are pregnant in your first trimester. Yes, my butt was pregnant. Within my 6 week after having our daughter I was having another. Let me tell you, I was so in shock and I don't know why because my boyfriend and I both had sex without a condom. I seriously was in shock and in denial. I was in denial that I was pregnant with my 3rd child. After years of saying and thinking I was in denial I thought about it. I was shocked at my actions that I wasn't ready financially.

    I wanted so much more than what I had

(my dreams) for my family. Now that I was ready to have another blessing I just knew it would be harder but I said "Thank you God for another angel from you". When I felt that little kick I stopped, and touched my belly and held it. It was a great feeling but then I said I can't be pregnant. My boyfriend said "Girl, you need to go to the doctors because you are pregnant". I went and they did a sonogram we were having a baby and I was blessed yet again. The funniest thing about finding out and telling my son that he's having another sibling.

This little boy reaction was with a straight face and he was 6yrs old "Mannnn, another one. That's a lot mom"! I felt so bad but I laughed and I told that story to my friends and family and they just laugh. I think that he loved that we were together for 5 yrs. before other people needed my attention. This little boy and I been through alot together and he has my heart and I wanted to spoil him rotten because he didn't have his dad and it wasn't his fault at all.

I wanted him to have a man to look up to and teach him how to grow up and be a great man. I could only do as much as I could. I love my son with every being in my body and I want the best for him. I wanted me and my boyfriend to raise this big family and just love one another and put God first. He loved my son and I could tell my son loved him. They never had a bad moment. My boyfriend whole family accepted me in with open arms and it felt great.

What would change the fact that we are doing the best that we could in God's walk to raise this family? I thought nothing. Every couple has problems and I knew we could get through ours. It wasn't a lot of them. We were a great couple with loving families on both sides. My family loved my man and took to him so quick.

My grandparents love him so much and it's more than what he would ever know. My granddad always asked how my man was doing anytime I talked to him. My grandmother would do the same. She would always tell us to pray and keep God first in our life. I was doing a lot of that because I knew we were going to be together forever. Me pregnant with my third baby and having a newborn and a 6 yr. old and going through hard times we broke up.

Starting over is hard to do

That hurt me so bad. I was so in love with him and my son loved him. I was hurt more that we were parting ways and I would disappoint my kids and being a single mother again. I prayed to God, stayed in church even though going through things in life. I was so close to God and just took my kids and moved out of the home we were living in together. It was my home and my least was up that's why I moved and I felt like this a change and I just wanted something different. I missed my place because my kids and I could just walk up the street to my grandparents' home.

Their health was concerning but they were always fighters and I knew they would live to be an old age. I wanted my kids to have that bond with my grandparents like I did. My kids and I would make sure we would go and see them every day. Soon as my kids and I moved about 25 minutes away it was a little more difficult to just stop and go see them. I made sure I would talk to them on the phone every day though. Still working and going to school and taking care of my kids and our home was hard but I tried my best and maintained it.

My son was the man of the house and I told him this. He like that because he said he will take care of us. He love his little sister and would play with her all the time while she crawls around the house. She was a little rat, so quiet and you would think that she's in one place and she would be in another. I would remember that my son would come wherever I would be and say "mom, I can't find Amanie". That would scare the mess out of me and the whole time he would know where she is. I would be walking around the house looking and she would be in the same place but really quiet because he brother would tell her to be quit.

How could a little tiny girl just sit in one spot and not say a word until I found her. When I do find her and say "There you are" with excitement she would laugh and my son I would grab and tackle him to the floor with laughs telling him "You tricked me again". These two had me occupied all the time with fun but I was still missing my ex. I was alone for a while but yes he tried to come back but I just knew it would be the same old thing we broke up for and nothing would change. I was scared because not only my heart would be affected but my babies would have to deal with losing a father again. Looking into my son face when my ex and I broke up had me so broken and I never wanted to see that again, ever. I was so upset with my ex that I said I wouldn't let him know when I go in labor with our 2nd daughter.

That's not right but I said I wouldn't but my family was so close with him I knew that he would know. He continued to tell me that he's not with anyone and I wanted to trust him but things that happen in the dark always come to light. That it did! So here I am going into labor and in my mind still saying I'm not telling him anything. In pain and my two cousins are with me Tierra and Sharita at the hospital. The two little girls I talked about earlier when I came home from Germany.

Well they were young ladies that grew up to be beautiful like I knew they would. They would laugh at me when I would say don't tell my ex anything about the baby coming. I'm lying in bed while having a contraction my door opens and guess who the hell walks in??? You know it! My ex and I wanted to get mad but that contraction was kicking my butt. He come over and try to console me and it made me feel better yes it did but I was very upset with him. I just wanted him to get it right. I never told him that but I was happy to see him.

    I just couldn't give in so easy and his mind wasn't ready for a family. He was there to see his beautiful daughter be blessed in this world and God made her perfect. He was there for a while holding her and just staring at her. I could see the love on his face for her and I could feel it from him. He loved his kids and I could tell it hurt him that he wasn't there every day with them but I just wasn't having it. He came over to me to kiss me and rub my head but lol yes I played hard.

I had to do this so that I could get over him eventually. He then left the hospital but one thing I can say about this man is he stayed in his kid's life and anything they needed (because i wouldn't have it no other way). I never had to ask his parents would be the first to give for all my kids even myself. He was always a great father. We just wasn't working out. My daughter was just a beautiful little baby with a full head of hair, and big beautiful eyes. She was a 6lb baby and very quit. She just fussed if she wanted a bottle or her diaper was messy. I was blessed to have 3 kids and all were very healthy.

    I was blessed and that made me happy but still so much was missing in my life. I came home to my babies so they could meet there little sister and the smiles on their faces. We now have a little Daeshaun 6, Amanie 11mths & our newest member little Ayriana my pride and joys. I sat on the chair and they both came and sat beside me while I pulled back her pink blankets. Daeshaun smiled and asked a lot of questions like can they stay in my room for that night as a family. That touched my heart and I said yes.

    He was happy and ran and put his blanket in my room while Amanie was examining her little sister and Daeshaun came back out to talk to his little sister. Amanie the whole time was touching her legs, her feet, her little fingers and her eyes. It was funny to see what she was doing because she was still not 1 yet. See I had my girls in the same year. One was born in January and the other in December. I'm blaming it all on him….ha-ha no I'm not (It was me also). All I did was take pictures of us and I felt so good.

    My babies all were happy and I was home with them taking great care of them. I made a vowel that I would just live and not think of my ex and leave it as it is. I still had love for him but he knew I was done with him. It was something that I knew we both needed and If sometime in life then it may work but not at this time. I had to raise my babies and work was definitely a part of it. I hated when I had to go to work and leave them.

    The best part of the end of the day was coming home to a peaceful home with my babies. Raise them in the way my grandparents raised me going to church and introducing my babies to God at an early age. I would sing gospel around the house all the time and they would sing with me. It was peaceful for sure. My ex parents would watch the kids for me while I was at work. They would feed them, get them ready for bed and when I get there everything would be done.

    I really appreciated them for that. I changed jobs and the hours were different so they couldn't watch my kids any longer but they were there with anything I need and they made that very clear. If I needed anything for all 3 of my kids they would do the best but definitely help me out. They kept their word throughout the years. So now It was me and my babies and work was great, I was getting my certifications for my job and things was awesome. I still was feeling lonely and I wanted some time going out on a date. I thought at least should be able to feel special as a woman.

    Everything that I been through with these guys when all I ever wanted was marriage, kids and to be happy. I never thought I would be this far in life with me still having in the back of my mind that horrible rape and that abusive relationship and being cheated on for no reason of my doing. I thought about that often even when I tried to see the happy moments in my life. My cousin wife called me one day and we were just talking on the phone and she knew what I been through. So I was telling her that I think I may want to go on a date to feel special for a change. I just wanted to stop thinking of these men that hurt me and in different ways.

She said well you should and then I said "naw, I don't! I'll just be content with my kids and just deal with what I put myself into. She laughed because of the way I said it and she said live for you, no one else. She told me call this guy and eventually I did. I don't know why I did it but I did and we talked on the phone for a very long time. He connected with me quick and me with him but I had kids so I wasn't giving in that easy. We were going to take everything very slow.

At this time my car died on me and he was willing for me to use his car while he's at work. I had things to do and I thought that was sweet of him. He would come over early in the morning and I would take him to work. This went on for a while (about 6 months) and we just became a couple. He knew that I was very independent and I never asked for anything. I went without many times and that's just was me.

This made me stronger because I had to do what I needed to survive and give to my babies. Everyday he would leave $200 up under the visor in the car. I saw it one day and called him and asked him why he would leave money open like that. He told me it's for me if I ever need it. I told him that I really appreciated it but ok and thank you. He would leave that amount and more sometimes every single day.

I never used it, not once. He was a good guy and always was there for my kids and myself. We were everywhere together and he bonded with my kids and I was really comfortable with it. He didn't have any kids of his own and if he wanted a child why would I hold that away from him. He had to be talking marriage for that and he surely was. My youngest was spoiled and she always wanted him. He called her "Mikey". That's because she ate everything.

We didn't plan on having more kids right away though. Everyone I met on his side of the family was nice except a couple. I don't know why because I am a very nice person. All I ever done was help anyone that needs it. I helped him a lot but he told me that it was because he stopped being there for them and giving money and they think that he's giving all to me (not true). He said to me "you help me out so don't worry about them".

After that I just I stayed away and if I had to be around I was just respectful (hi, bye). I don't like being around negative people and yes I will just stay away. At this time in my life my new man was being that man that I need and for me I was still trying to step back and let my man be the man in our relationship. It is hard when that's all you know is to handle everything and be independent. I wanted to be the type of woman that has her own and having a husband would just be a blessing and what God put together. I tried to step down and give some of my stress to my man but it was very hard.

Now, sometime has passed and I was happy with my family and my kids were happy and that was the most important part in my life that I wanted to feel. A year has gone by and my boyfriend wanted to make it official and move in together. I thought about it and I felt like this is my time. No more being afraid of being alone. Just a single mother with 3 kids and I always felt I had to watch my back because I brought along my past hurt and fears. I didn't want anyone to hurt me physically or mentally again and I would have an extra body that loved us and would protect us. So I agreed and we went looking together for a home.

My least was going to be up very soon and we had to hurry. Well by the time it was up we still didn't find anything that we wanted for our family. I didn't know what to do. The bills was getting up there for me and I was handling it but barely. I had a choice. Either I stay and stress about my bills or do something temporary. I didn't like either but I did what I thought I should. You know what I forgot to do???

I didn't pray on it and wait till GOD guide me in the right direction. I end up moving with an aunt and I really appreciated her and my uncle because they took in me with 3 kids and just finding out I was pregnant with my 4th child. I always asked my kids their opinion on having another brother or sister but I learned from my oldest (don't ask). I love it though because this gave my kids a voice to express their feelings. At this time my Granddad was going through a lot and was in an assisted living facility. His doctor didn't find out right away that he had diabetes and he was having a lot of leg pain.

He ended up getting one of his legs amputated and again the doctors cut below his knee and had to go back and cut above his knee. He had told me before that it's crazy but he would get up in the middle of the night with pain in his leg. He would go to grab his leg and it wasn't there. We went to see him often though and Grandma was still in the house on the end row but a family member was helping care for her. When I moved in with my aunt a few doors down and Grandma knew every day I would see her. I loved it and my baby's did also.

She would come over in the morning, every morning and we would watch television together. I would prepare her lunch and we would eat together and just enjoy each other's company while watching the stories that came on 12noon like. Like Guiding Light. This was the best for me because I always wanted to stay very close in my Grandparents life. My Grandmother was there always and when I went into labor with my 4th child she was there the whole time. I only wanted to lay in her arms until the pain of the contractions went away and still I laid there. She would rock me, sing to me and pray and it eased my mind and took me back to where I felt peace.

If anyone would try to rub my back, my feet or whatever it just made my contractions so much worst. The time had come for me to give birth to my fourth child. All I could think about is getting into our home together as a family and just live our happy life (I was hoping). Getting up from holding my grandma arms so tight because I wanted her to go with me to the hospital. She told me that she would be waiting for me when I come back home with my baby. My Aunt Sylvia and my cousin Tierra husband Eric picked me up and put me in the car. I couldn't walk for anything I was in pain.

    My son was born later that day and I called my grandmother to let her know. He voice was always just like heaven sent. The delivery went well and I had a healthy little boy. His father was at the hospital the whole time and brought me back to my aunt's home where I was staying. I would've loved coming home to my family in my own home but this is what life gave me and I took it. No later than a couple of months if that we ended up moving.

    I believe at this time my Grandmother had fell and broke a bone in her leg. My grandmother had surgery and had to go to an assisted facility until she healed. The same one my Granddad was staying in. I was happy to know they were together once again. He was able to go and see my grandma at his leisure and he went to see her every day. I loved that they could still see one another everyday but I hated that they had to be in an assisted facility. It just wasn't home and I didn't think that they would get great treatment.

I was wrong but I couldn't have what I wanted like back in the day because everyone was getting older. My 4 kids, my man and myself moved and it was a great feeling. I prayed over this house and I knew this was home for now. I was working fulltime with my 4th child Davon until I started having lots of complications and my doctor put me on bed rest. I didn't listen because that's what I knew to do is take care of myself and my family and now that I have 4 kids I definitely couldn't rest.

Stop working…who me? I can't! I didn't hit any mega millions so my butt had to stay working for now. The baby didn't like it and my man said to me "I want you to take time off because I got us". I didn't like it but I had no choice and I started going to school for my high school diploma because I dropped out in the 12th grade. It was a lot I haven't told you how much my Grandmother meant to me this is it.

You know the childhood I been through and I always could count on my grandparents to protect me really. My grandma was more hands on with me than my granddad and he made sure we all were alright. I loved them both so much but grandma was the one that I saw praying, singing and praising wherever. I loved my grandmother more than God. I know what you may think about that but if you understand what I've been through since a little baby. What made me feel so safe was the flesh which I could run, call, touch or talk to her and I heard her voice. She taught me to go to God and talk to him and yes I was one to pray but I didn't give God time to talk to me

. I always intervened and that held me back from my blessings. I knew it wasn't right to put anyone or anything before God but I ran to what I felt real for a little girl that needed the flesh to feel safe. Growing up I prayed about it and talked to God and apologized and I felt that he forgave me. I know God knew what I needed but wanted me to come back to rely on him and I did. My grandma was my world and Since I was a teenager I would sit in my room and pray that God makes me stronger and stronger each day because I knew if my grandma passed away I wouldn't be able to live.

I would cry when the thought just crossed my mind. My grandmother would tell me also that one day she would go with God and I would always say "Grandma please stop talking about that".

When I moved out and didn't see my grandma every day, my kids and I would go to the facility visit her and granddad every week. Even if we couldn't stay long we did go say hi, give our love and bring them something always. We knew granddad always wanted pies and cigarettes he would get them from us. We loved going shopping for whatever granddad wanted and he always was very appreciative for the visits even though they weren't so long. When I brought my youngest son Davon to see granddad he said he's going to be a football star. He held him and said "Nique come get him, he's heavy".

He looked at Davon's hands and said he's going to be a big boy. He loved our visits and the kids had lots of questions that he didn't mind answering for them. My kids never got tired and never wanted to leave, they loved being around grandma and granddad. I was home with my kids and you know I didn't think I could do it but being home all the time taking care of the kids was great. I loved being a stay at home mom since I had a man that took control and was being the man that I believed God brought to my family. Even though I was with this other man my grandfather still asked about my ex (my girls father).

My grandparents would tell me to tell my ex they asked about him. I would say alright but I didn't see him much at all. My granddad told me that my ex came to see him a couple of times there. I was shocked about that.

So, Going home taking care of it and having my kids all the time is all I did. I wasn't going out not even spending time with my family much. I was a mommy that my time was spent around school which I kept putting off back and forth whenever I was going through something. I just couldn't concentrate much so I would wait until I could. I didn't know at this time my boyfriend was feeling some kind of way and he wanted me to go back to work. He often let things outside of home like the problems from work which he brought home and stayed distant.

    He never sat me down and talked about it as grown people. He would show attitude and I had no clue why. He really was going through something himself. When he got off of work I had dinner cooked and all he had to do was come in, take a shower, eat dinner and rest. Of course the kids would tackle him and want his time and he would give it to them and then he would go to the room. I kept the kids quiet and doing things with them that kept them chilled out but that was my kids anyway. All my kids was very quiet and they would play but you really didn't have to say "be quiet" or anything like that.

He had it good but I guess he wasn't making enough money or wanted more for some so maybe the job he had was giving him problems. I know he wanted to have his own company but that took more money and lot's more that he just couldn't give up at that time. He came out and said it in a way that I didn't like but I kept my cool and said that's all you had to do was talk with me. I started looking right away but now I had to find a sitter for all my kids and I needed to trust whoever it was. I ended up getting a job that I didn't like but it was the first thing that came along. Ok so are you ready to laugh??

I was the person behind the counter in the grocery store asking how much lunchmeat you want. Yes, I was cutting meat in a grocery store so that I could keep my relationship together. I'm not downgrading anyone that does that but for me no one I knew could see me doing that. I could barely see over the counter itself I was so short. It was what God gave me and I took it. I didn't have time to go back to what I loved and that was taking care of the elderly in an assisted living facility. I had to wait for the call so I could go back to the same job I had before I was put on bed rest.

    I could tell from him he didn't want me to wait so I did this job until something else came through. Now, I was tired all the time but I had to deal with 4 kids getting, dinner, and house cleaned and getting them bathed and in bed. Not him, so I would fall out when I had the chance to. That's when I would get that I'm cheating. This was a total shock to me and I did whatever I could to ease his mind. I go to the grocery store but when I come back stressed because I have little ones with me and it's taking longer that it should to go shopping. He would be home but I don't even say anything I would just take my babies wherever I go.

I never cared because I am their mommy and I brought them in this world so I had to take care of them. This thing with me being out there or talking to someone ended up getting really bad. One day I went to my father's to get away from feeling so down. Just to get a smile on my face I just knew when I go back that it wouldn't be good. My cell was broke and I didn't have an extra one so my father told me to take his phone just in case I needed it. I told him that I would be fine.

I will just go in the house and do what I normally would do just be quiet. So my kids wanted to stay with my father that night except the baby and he wanted to keep them. I ended up taking my father's phone and I took my baby boy home with me. This attitude that my man was giving me just wasn't him and I didn't know what was going on. So I went home and I was in the living room with my baby who was fast asleep lying next to me on our couch. In the dark just watching television until I fell asleep myself.

I heard a key in the door and my heart started racing because I was scared that he would come in and want to fuss for no reason. I had my night clothes on and I was just home bored to death but was watching television until I fell asleep. So he came in and said nothing to me. It was pitch black in the house except for the television in the living room. He walked right in, heading to the back and never turned on a light. I followed him with my eyes until I couldn't see him anymore.

In my thoughts I was wondering why he wouldn't turn on a light to see. Then I thought ok, he maybe that tired and he's just going to go to sleep. I was going to wait until I thought he would be knocked out then I would go to bed. I hate arguing and especially when it doesn't make any since because I'm a faithful woman. I believe what you do to others it comes back and bites you harder. God just doesn't like evil.

I am just not that type of woman that keeps or even have drama around. One of my nicknames was "SMILEY" for a reason. Then all of a sudden he comes from out of the dark and walk towards the door. I spoke and he said nothing to me. I just hunched my shoulder whatever and continued to watch television just feeling that tonight is going to be weird but I will get through it.

He comes back like 7 minutes later with something in his arm and it was really long but under a coat. I thought it was a shot gun but I was wondering why he would hide it under a coat. I went to look at his face and I couldn't see it. What I mean is that it was his body but the face area was black and not because it was dark in the house. I saw his face the other times barely but I felt that it was a spirit in him taking over and I followed him with my eyes again thinking should I get the heck out of here. I knew that you can't show a spirit fear because that's when they mess with you.

    I'm still watching him and then he disappears in the dark and not one time would he turn on the light so that he can see. I took my father phone and hid it under the couch and turned it off. He knew that I didn't have a phone right now so I wanted him to continue to think that so I hid it just in case I needed it. I picked my baby up and held him close in my arms. He ended up going out the door again and when he did that I took my baby in the back and turned on every light in that house. I went in the room laid my baby in his bed and ran to his side to see if it was a gun that he brought back in the house.

When I was looking under the bed I heard him coming in so I leaped across the bed so quick and laid in the bed like I was going to sleep. I didn't want to make like I was leaving and things would not have went good. I been in a situation like this so I didn't want my life gone in the hands of a man for no reason and my babies would live in this world without me. I thought we would just not speak to one another and get up the next morning and get back on the right track. I know that not every relationship is perfect so I didn't mind working on it. Well by me getting scared and taking that leap over the bed my heart was pounding so hard I thought he could hear it.

    He came back in and I was just lying in the bed facing my son but I could see the door. He started turning off the lights and I made sure that I looked him in his face so I could see him again. I did and that made me feel better just a little. He gets in the bed and my heart is going for it. I thought that it was vibrating the whole bed I was so nervous. So it's dark in the house again he gets in the bed and I'm just looking around with my eyeballs like what is he doing. I thought he was facing the window opposite to me.

    He came out of the nowhere and said "you cheater". I didn't say anything and continued to lay there. He was so close to the back of my head I felt his breath on my neck and I was getting chills. If he puckered up with his lips he would've kissed me on my neck but he kept saying it and I was getting very upset. Then he called me a "bitch" and kept saying it so I said very calmly "I'm not a bitch and I never cheated on you". Why did I talk at all?

    The next thing I know he started kicking me out of the bed literally with his feet. Every time he would kick me and I would fall out of the bed I would just get my butt back in it. I didn't want to stand to my feet then I felt like

I would have to fight and my baby was there. I still remember if I need anyone I just have to get to the couch and get that phone. By kicking me off the bed wasn't working for him then he gets off the bed and lifts it up in the air so I could fall off. This made me almost fall on my baby and that's when I completely lost it.

    I jumped up and started going off on him yelling and I looked at my baby that was still sleep and I calmed down quick. I didn't want anything to happen to me or my baby so I he ran all up in my face getting loud and still calling me names. I walked away to the bathroom to get away from him and tried to close it before he got there but he was on my back. He told me to get out of the house. I'm thinking, don't you know that I have 4 kids and you told me to stop working cause you got us. I let down my guard because I felt that you had my back so I could continue to work toward my goal of finishing school and I have your back but you are telling me to get out. My name is on this least also so I'm not going anywhere. He started pushing me and I said "I'm not leaving my baby".

I only had on a tank top and very tiny shorts that showed the bottom of my butt because I was in my home, in my bed. He was making it very hard for me to get my baby so I grabbed my flip flops and the phone was right beside them, so I grabbed that quickly also. I still was trying to get my baby boy but he was handling me and I couldn't do anything because he pushed me out the door. Now it's very early in the morning like about 2am and it doesn't look right that I'm out there with tiny shorts on. First I called my cousin Tierra and she called our cousin Sharita. I told them what was going on and just come get me please.

Then I called my father and he was on the way that quick. He was close to where I live. I had cars driving by me whistling at me, yelling at me and I just knew someone was going to get me before anyone of my family would get there. My father got there really quick so I walked to the street so they could see me. I'm just sitting there while waiting for my father wondering what is it about me that I have to go through this. I had called my cousin also because I needed someone come to get me ASAP.

My father showed up first and I actually forgot that I was talking to my cousin Tierra. So my father and step-mother Sharon picked me up from the side of the road. They asked where was the baby and I told them that he wouldn't let me get my baby and forced me out of the house. So we went back to the house. Before he forced me out every light was on in the house again and now every light was off. I didn't have a key but I told them what I thought I saw in his jacket when he was going in and out of the door.

I just didn't want anyone going in there

and that was a gun and he just flipped out and started shooting. So we are at the door and my father asked me do I have a key. I said no and he locked the door behind me. My father tried the door and it opened up. I said "I'm not going in there, he may kill us all". My father walked in and had the door wide open.

My father called out my boyfriend's name and he didn't answer. He was loud and he got louder and called his name again. No answer so my father started walking to the bedroom. I was thinking like you better come back before he take your head off. My stepmother and I was at the door waiting for him to talk. My father turned on the lights and said "Why are you sitting here in the dark.

Where is the baby and then he said "Nique, come get the baby". I walked down the hall into the room slowly and I picked my baby up and he was just sitting on the bed not saying anything. I grabbed what I could quickly and got the heck out of there. My father was talking to him and I'm not sure what he said but it had something to do with me and the kids and how could he do this to his family. We ended up leaving and we got to my father's house talked about it to them because they wanted to know what set him off. I still can't tell you to this day what switched in his head.

Maybe he seen all those kids in the house at once but he said he loved the kids and they never wasn't a problem. He said before coming into the house it was hard to believe that we had 4 kids and it was that quiet. I tell you I don't know but he must have been going through something and he act out in that way. So my kids and I stayed at my father's house then I get a call from my cousin Tierra asking me where I was. I forgot about her and she had the crew up there ready to get busy. I told her that my father came to get me.

She said that she came up to my house

with my Aunt Rita, Aunt Felita and my cousin Sharita and with some things of their own. They went to the door and they were banging. He came to the door and they asked him where was I. He told them that I was gone and they didn't believe him. They told him he better open that door now or else. He never opened the door but he said to them that my father came and picked up me and the baby. They had to verify before they left thinking I was in there and he hurt me.

    I let them know that my kids and I was fine and with my father and they went home. We was together for a while and craziness happened. I tell you If I was at fault in any way I wouldn't have a problem saying it but I did nothing wrong to him. He stayed there and told me I had to get out so he told me to come and get my things out. I checked some things out to see if he could do that. We ended up going to court and I told the judge just what happen.

He told his side of the story and the judge told me that I get to keep the place and he had to leave. The judge also gave him every other weekend with his son and told him that he had to pay child support. I was happy but I thought about it. I wasn't working much and he had a lot to do with that because even after I got another job he wanted me to leave that also. In my head he was trying to make me into a house wife. That's what was happening anyway really but I'm the one that wanted to go back to work and he told me to wait and just raise the kids because they need me home.

When the judge granted everything I left there and went to the house so that I could get his things out and my home back in order. Police had to be there though to make sure everything went well. I get there and open the door all my things and my kids' things were in the middle of the living room floor like I was getting put out. Oh, I see this dude thought that

I was headed out the door and it was him that had to leave. All of this craziness kept me from going to see my grandparents as often as I was. They could tell I was going through something but I kept that from them.

    He removed all of his things out and I had a peaceful home and it felt good to not have to come home and be worried about fussing or anything negative. It was lonely because someone that again I thought was God sent and my final forever was no longer. It was hard to handle the bills there because he was taking care of everything except the food and my car insurance but I was literally living paycheck to paycheck with 4 kids. I couldn't keep this place alone and I didn't want to move anyone in with me. I just decided again to pick up with my kids even if I had to start over again. This time I started getting really depressed and felt like why couldn't I just be happy with the love of my life?

Why after 4 kids I wasn't married yet and the men that came in my life I brought their kids into this world and still they went crazy. I started thinking something was wrong with me but I did everything I could but to be a fool with them and I just didn't settle. I had a conversation with my Aunt Nadine who I cherish dearly and trust in her words. Without me saying this to her she came out the blue and said to me "Dominique, don't think that something is wrong with you". She was one that always told me to pray and talk to God and let him guide me. I did that and I noticed that I would always try to help out and we know that you can't try and help God out at all.

God would stop and let you go on and put yourself in your situation, but he will be there for you when you are ready to give it all to him.

I was in a really bad place at this time

and I didn't know what to do. Now I did something that I shouldn't have and that was go backwards. Yup, my girl's father was always around my family and I don't remember when we ended up talking again but he came to my home one day and he told me that he's sorry for everything that happen. He said that it was his fault that I was going through all of this and He wants to be the Godly man in me and my kids life. I trusted him again and we started hanging out again. Things started going up in my life.

I got my job back and I was still trying to finish school but I ended up getting my license to be a CNA's, and Got Med certified to distribute medication anywhere I want to work in the nursing field. I was back with my girl's father whom I wanted from the beginning and was praying that this work out great.

Well kept secret

It was and one day a few months passed and my stepmother Sharon asked me a question and I laughed. She asked me am I pregnant. I knew I was gaining weight but I knew that was stress and me eating out a lot because of my schedule with work and school. No way could I be. I went to get check out by my doctor and behold we was having our 3rd baby together. He was ecstatic and I didn't know how to feel. I was afraid that I would have to bring another baby in this world and he would act an ass again. I said to myself I need to get fixed. I mean don't get me wrong I always wanted a huge family with my husband but that's what was missing (a husband). I told him I just couldn't do this. He begged for me to keep it and I told him no. I found out that he was seeing someone and he didn't leave that situation alone before coming back to me. It was a mess on their part and I didn't want anything to do with that. I didn't need to go to jail and I had kids here that I brought into this world. I wanted to get an abortion but I fought myself on it so much. I asked my Aunt to go with me and she tried to talk to me to make sure I knew what I was really doing. I just couldn't do it alone. He went MIA to make sure I didn't get this abortion and he wouldn't help me with getting the money. It was really hard for me but I did it and made sure my heart was closed down to where I wouldn't feel anything about doing this. This guy again was out of my life and I am getting tired of this back and forth but how do you shut off loving someone….. You have to be completely done and fed up but until then you just keep putting yourself in these crazy emotions. It's not his fault it's ours because we really have the upper hand on how our life should go.

    God showed up so I was able to move back to the area I grew up in. My kids and I was just fine and happy. Yes I felt alone because I didn't have a companion but I knew that if I waited God would bring me my husband. All I did was work and come home to my babies. My kids and I still visit grandma and granddad. The times that my kids and I was home we would have movie night until we saw our first Tyler Perry play "Madea".

Oh it was then that we fell in love with his plays and every single time it came out we was one of the first to buy it. I would be excited and they would laugh at me because I would be rocking. Thanks to my Aunt Rita who manage homes she had one for me and my babies. So while my babies and I were going to visit our grandparents and the visits was always a pleasure and we loved seeing each other. One day the kids and I went for a visit and we saw granddad first and then went to visit Grandma.

Everyone in the family was talking how grandma was getting Alzheimer's and she would talk about family that passed on. I knew that I didn't want to witness that because it just would hurt me really bad and I couldn't see my grandmother in that way. So I was kind of dreading to see her and hear her talk in that state of mind. So they kids and I was on the elevator and they were ahead of me and when they turn the corner they said "mom, I see grandma". I turn the corner and all I saw was grandma smiling very big.

I wanted to cry of happiness just seeing her smiling like that. The kids ran to her and gave her kisses and hugs and I did the same thing. She said all of my kid's names and she knew mine. We hugged so long I'm not sure if I was holding her or she was holding on to me longer. I sat with her and we talked about me and the kids and again she asked about the girl's father. I told her that I don't like him and he's mean and she said "aww Nique he's a good guy". Not what he put me through Grandma and she would just give me a smile.

The kids and I would stay until grandma and granddad would get tired. I just never wanted to leave them. So I had to leave for some reason this day so we gave grandma so much love, kisses and hugs. I held on to her a little longer this time and we started to leave. I told her that I love her so much and I should just wheel her out of the facility with us and she laughed at me. So the elevator was just around the corner and the kids was racing to push the down button and I was telling them to be careful.

    While I was walking away just before I hit the corner I turned and looked back at grandma and the look on her face was so priceless. She gave me a smile but her eyes was saying so much and I blew her a kiss and mouthed I love you so much and she blew me a kiss and the elevator opened. My heart felt so heavy but I had to rush off. I told my kids that I should just go get grandma and granddad and take them with us. I thought about her look the whole day but I knew that I would see her again soon. I actually was going to see her in a few days and I couldn't wait to see her smile and granddad the way he greets us when we came to see him.

The moment I couldn't breathe & my world turned around

A couple days later I was home watching television with my kids and it was just a normal day. I get a phone call from my cousin Carlet. She says to me "What are you doing?" I answered "Nothing" and she says "We have to get to the hospital because they found grandma in bed and she wasn't responding". I jumped quickly to my feet but something eased my mind. Carlet said I'm going to come and get you. She hung up and called me back within 2 minutes and told me to hurry up we have to get to the hospital right away.

I'm feeling like why is she rushing because I know that grandma was going to be alright. So my aunt Evon came to my house and said that she would watch my kids for me until I came back. I get to the hospital and walk in the door to the ER and I see no one I recognize. My cousin Carlet told me that we had to go through the other doors because the family is waiting in this room. So we go through the doors and I see lots of the family. I'm assuming that they are there because we don't know what's going on and they let the family in the back.

I sit in the room and look around at everyone's face. The looks was disturbing but I said I will not feel any kind of way because we have no clue what's going on. We sat here for about an hour but I don't know really and all of a sudden a doctor walks in the door and everyone was quit and looking his way. He begin to say "Your mother came in from the facility where one of the nurse's aide found her unresponsive. They were doing their rounds and she wasn't responding to anything so they called 911 and the ambulance brought her here. We worked on her longer than we normally would but I'm sorry to say she didn't make it". My Aunt Rita let out this scream and I heard cries, and everything.

    I looked at my father and he looked at me then the doctor said "We can let a couple people at a time back to see her". I was the first to say "I want to go" first. I looked at my father but I guess I was in denial because I didn't cry. I felt numb and needed to see for myself before I went along with everyone else. I said when I was younger that if my grandma ever passed away I would lose it and probably have to go in a hospital or something because it was like our hearts was intertwined together. I use to feel sharp pains in my chest and I would call my grandma.

    It was her having tightness in her chest

but I would feel them as well. I was in total shock because I felt that they had it wrong. They just need to go back where they had her and keep working. My Aunt Maxine and her husband Uncle Walter walked down with me. We were the first to go in and see her. When the doctor walked through the door where they had her body (I felt fear). It was fear of really seeing her gone away from us.

 I was scared to death because I was always scared to see a dead body and what it may look like. My Aunt Sylvia told me a long time ago that it's not the dead that we should be scared or afraid of, it's the living. That made since to me but it was a little weird to see someone with no life in them. This wasn't just someone man this was my heart, my life, and my everything and this doctor is telling me that she's no longer here with us. So we are in the room and they had dim lights and I held on to my Aunts arm until I actually looked at my grandma. She looked as if she was just sleep. I was kind of shocked because she had color to her and she was warm.

They said she was gone when she was at the facility but they worked on her in the ambulance and in the hospital. She was already gone when my cousin called me the first time to tell me we have to go to the hospital because of grandma and I didn't know this. I walked up to the bed where grandma was laying and broke down. I laid my head right under her neck where I always laid on her. My noise was in the crease of her neck and I laid there for the longest time crying. I never wanted to move from that spot. I didn't know but everyone was coming in and out but all I knew is that I wanted my grandmother to get up and say "I'm alright".

I wasn't getting up until I heard her voice. All of a sudden I felt her move and I jumped up and looked at her but it was my cousin Tierra who came in and she wanted to see if it was true also. I said "T did you feel that, Grandma just moved". She said "No, that was me". I then fell back into grandma's neck and laid there with tears falling down her neck. When I finally got up no one was there in the room with us and I said to her. I said "grandma, that day that I blew a kiss at you and you gave me a look. That was your goodbye to me"? She didn't answer but I felt that's what she was saying. I wanted to come back to see you grandma and I'm so sorry I didn't stay longer.

    I felt that my time was cut very short with her and I was angry. Grandma was my life, my air, my everything and I didn't want to keep praying for strength all those years because I felt that he would make me strong just for this day that I didn't want to come true. That was the last day that I would be able to actually be able to touch my grandmother, to hear her voice and see her again ever in life.

Everyone said that we had to go and tell granddad because the only thing that he knew was grandma was unresponsive and was rushed to the hospital. I knew I had to be there no matter what. So a huge group of us went back to the facility where grandma and granddad lived.

We all got off the elevator together and walked into his room. His bed was next to the window so I fit into a space at the end of the bed beside him and the window. Everyone gathered into the room and we kissed him and my Aunt Rita told him that momma didn't make it. Granddad said "oh momma" but just those words he spoke hurt me because I knew his pain. I went home that day and cried my eyes out. My eyes were so sore to the touch and wipe because that's all I've been doing.

I didn't want to do anything but lay in bed for the rest of my life. My life just seemed so not worth living at that time because MY MOTHER….she was gone, passed on, in heaven she was no longer on this earth with me to talk to, to cry on, to laugh with my everything was gone. I talked to God and I told him how I felt I wasn't mad with him but I needed her here with me. I always told my mom that I have to pass on before her because I wouldn't be able to make it without her. She knew this that's why she always told me to pray for strength.

I love that woman so much and to this day November 30, 2014 @5:29pm I sit here crying like she just passed on. It's still hard for me but no one knows because I keep this to myself and In the privacy of my room looking at her picture never wanting to forget her looks, her touch, her smile, her laughter and most of all her prayers. She passed away February 11, 2005 and the next few days was the worst for the family. Everyone had to go on with their everyday life of working and it was hard for all. I just couldn't go into work. My heart was really tore up and all I did was cry.

I knew that I wanted to give my grandma something special from my heart so I wrote her a note. When I was younger in school we had to right about someone in our life that was our hero and I wrote about my grandma. Well I needed to write this and ask can it be in her obituary. Her funeral was on Thursday February 17, 2005. We were Christians so she had a Christian wake 9am until 10am and the funeral started at 10:30am. Walking into our home church and the first thing you see is a casket at the front open with my mom laying in it was so so so hard. I walked up to her and saw her laying there in my favorite color (light sky blue) and I believe the casket was the same color.

So, when I get to her I just bend down and tell her I love her and kiss her on her cheek then broke down. My Aunt Nadine walked up to me and held me and then I sat right where

I could see her in the very first row. I wanted to keep my eye on my mom until they closed the casket. This day was so hard for everyone and when I saw my father bring my granddad there and I watched granddad look at grandma in that casket was something I never wanted to see. My heart was breaking more and more. I tried to be strong for whomever needed me but I couldn't be strong for myself.

All I did was burst out in tears all through the service. My cousin Tierra came and sat by me and just held me close and we cried together. See she was my little cousin but family that close also feel like sisters and she did live with us for a short period of time. We were close but I was close with all of my cousins. My cousin Michelle Jones sang a solo and it was just beautiful. I just couldn't take it and I got up to go to the bathroom.

I didn't look up until I got to the end of the church pews and I saw standing up on the wall my ex (my girl's father). He was there for us and I loved him even more for this. He paid his respect to my mom and I tell you she loved him so much. When I came out of the bathroom my father was there and asked me was I alright. I said yes because I was trying to hold strong but broke down right there in his arms. My father held me until I was ready to go back out there.

I did and sat down. My cousin Rosey was reading the Obituary and my letter to my grandmother was ready to be read. This was a special thank you letter to my grandma and I was happy that it would be read in front of her and I knew she was listening and hugging me at this time.

A Special Thanks to my Grandma.......

To the most beautiful woman in the world. I'm so happy that I got the chance to let you know how happy you made my life. You are an inspiration to me and my everything! I thank God so much he sent me to this beautiful family. With the two strongest Angels you and Granddad. You were there for my every cry and emotion and I yearn to hear those words again "(Nique I am here for you but first pray and give it to God)". You heard it all from me. You became my best friend when I started walking up through my teens and it will continue on. I will always love you! You gave me something special that no one will understand. It's the strongest love I have ever felt. You are my inspiration and the reason for living. For years I started praying to God to keep me strong for this day. The day you have been telling me about. I'm extremely sad, but also glad you got your prayers answered. I am strong because of you. Thanks Grandma for everything. You are my angel of love and my hero.

Just keep a seat for me in heaven next to you.

I love you,

Your baby Nique

This also was in my grandma obituary …….

You'll Never Walk Alone

"Safely Home"

I am home in heaven dear one.

Oh so happy and so bright

There is perfect joy and beauty in this everlasting life,

And pain and grief, are over, so safely home in heaven at last.

Did you wonder why, I so calmly trod the valley of shade?

Ah! But Jesus loved illumined (give life) every dark and fearful glade.

And he came himself to meet me in that way so hard to tread,

And with Jesus arms to lean on,

Could I have no doubt or dread?

Then you must not greed so sorely, for I love you dearly still.

Try to look beyond earth's shadows, pray to trust the Gathers will.

There is work still waiting for you, so you must not idly stand.

Do it now while life remaineth, you should rest in Jesus land.

When that work is all completed, he will gently call you home

On the rapture of that meeting.

Oh, the Joy to see you come.

    We buried my grandmother. When leaving the grave site was the test on how to go on with one of our angels that held the family together was gone. Now we had to keep granddad in good spirits and keep him uplifted. Granddad got visits all of the time and my kids and I was there more often now seeing him and him still being a part of my kid's life seeing them grow up. When I told my kids that we were going to see granddad they would say "and don't forget to go to the store and get his chocolate cakes mom". Granddad always smiled when my crew and I came to see him. He would say "Nique you love me don't you"?

I would say "Yes Sir with a smile and he would say "I know you do and you bring granddad all the goodies lol". If he was in bed when we get there he would get up, put all his clothes on and we would go outside for a while. Granddad would stroll around and introduce us to the staff (he was in a wheel chair). He was always proud of his family.

I remember him talking about Sherman Jr. all the time because he was so proud of him.

He always said that Sherman

(I call him Shermy) was going to be something great. Grandma and Granddad always knew that their grandkids had many talents and prayed upon them achieving them. My grandparents loved their family so much and those doing any & everything they need to do for them to help them always would.

Now at this time I was a single mother working hard to provide for my kids and myself but still all that I was going through my heart was love and I hated that. Why couldn't I just worry about me and my kids? Why did I feel for so many that hurt me? This was a gift that was passed down and the God that is within me. I was always one to pretty much stay to myself. I love my family to the moon and back and back to the moon again but I'm really reserved in many ways.

I was working in the nursing field and I

loved it. I was happy at this point in my life but still going through the tears and pain of losing my best friend (my grandmother). I barely talked to my kids' father because I didn't have to. Every now and again they would call and try to carry on a conversation and that was showing that they were still interested in me but my guards would stay up. Why wouldn't it? So, on a few occasions I would talk to my youngest son father and our conversations was the kids and how things are going.

One thing I knew about him is that no matter what he took care of the kids and home. He tried to be a good partner and was working on it. He didn't get over me completely and I thought about him often. He had moved into an apartment with a guy roommate but he said that he misses his family. Now I'm paying $1,250 a month for a townhome with 3 bedrooms 1 bathroom and 4 kids. This is not including bills like electric, phone, car insurance, gas.

Food…. I had to get help with feeding my growing babies it was tearing my pockets up. Food stamps is what I needed and was blessed to have. Yes, Sir I'll take that lol. So we talked a lot about him just moving back to my place because their lease was going to be up. He wanted to get his family back and he wasn't going to have a situation that he had to leave this man to pay extra bills. He didn't want to move to the area I was living but I had more room in my place.

He just had a 2 bedroom apartment, 2 full baths but we had 4 kids. I thought about how we could make it work with all the money I was bringing in and his job. The rent was no more than $900 so I knew this was going to be something great. I talked to my Aunt Rita and discussed to her what I thought would be a good idea because I was renting from her. I am one that may ask for advice only from a select few but I never take criticism the wrong way because I know they are saying what's right and what's wrong. My Aunt asked me am I sure?

I told her the only thing I can do is just try again because what I only wanted was a father for my kids that was respectful, loving, caring, for them no matter what. I chose to leave my home where my girls had their own princess room laid out beautiful. They had everything they wanted and I was very pleased with it. I left my home where my boys had their room where I purchased with my money a bunk bed worth $1,500 because I wanted to. They had their room laid out just like they wanted it and we all were very happy. I loved my peace with my babies and they loved having their happy mom playing, smiling and having fun with them.

So I chose to leave this for a chance to try out having something I have wanted my whole life and that's just a family. I picked up my family and moved with my youngest son father. Everything was so great! I am working but my commute was longer to get to work and get my babies to school. I did it though because I could and I wanted my babies to go to the same school. I always had Honor Roll kids and that made me absolutely a proud mom.

The holidays was great just like everyday was for us. My kids already knew the routine with being back in the house with my youngest son father but nothing change with my kids. They got home from school, did their homework while I gave them a snack and checked their work. They had chores and that was to be done first before outside time or just play time period. We ate dinner at 6pm and bath time was starting at 7pm. At this time my man dinner was done and all he had to do was come home to eat give us some quality time and then get rest.

This was something that went on for a whole year. I was content and thought this was going to be something great with our family. In the mist of living a good life, kids happy and the man and I was doing great it had to be something going wrong? I was in the dark about what he was going through. He kept a lot of stress in so the communication really wasn't there. We tried to hold on to our relationship and we did just that.

The kids kept him happy and I could tell when he would hit the door coming in from work and they all would yell out his name and his son would yell daddy. He would smile and embrace them. He would come in and a few times he would leave out after his shower, get dressed and put on some cologne. See one thing I knew about him was he wasn't the type to go out to clubs, bars he was just a hardworking man for his family and home. I started feeling like something just wasn't right and I would ask him who he was seeing and if there was someone else. He always said no but it was the way he said it.

Now, he had my mind wondering and I never like feeling that way. My past I wanted to keep just there but certain situations I was going through always brought it up in my head. I started feeling like he's just back to hurt me and I would play the fool. We started ignoring one another and barely talking but I knew this wasn't good for us and the kids feeling like something wasn't right. So we tried to sit and talk about what do we really want to do and we had to think about the babies. We wanted to work out and I think I wanted to work more than him but that's my feeling.

He may say he wanted to work more than I did but the crazy things is (it could've been true). One day the kids, my man and myself was all in the living room together talking and laughing and I stood up to do something. My man said to me "you are getting big". I looked at him like (really you are talking about me getting big) lol. He said "No really lift up your shirt". I looked at him with a weird look like why but I did and he burst out laughing.

    I smiled and said "What are you laughing at". He looked at me and said "You are pregnant". Now, I was afraid of getting pregnant because it was like I was just so dang on fertile and my Aunt Nadine and Aunt Felita would play with me and say that all the time. So I laughed myself and said "Ha, No I'm not and I can prove it. A matter of fact I have I have a test in the bathroom (I'll be right back)".

    Of course I am feeling very confident that I just need to lose some weight. The kids and I always hit a fast food restaurant if I was late getting home to cook dinner or we would have movie night with snacks. Ok I hate to exercise and wouldn't do it. So I know I was putting on a little something around the stomach. So I go into the bathroom and I hear the kids asking my man (are we having a sister or a brother)? I was in the bathroom like ha yeah right.

I knew that wasn't going to happen because I told my man that we need to start using condoms because I didn't want to pop up with another baby but he didn't mind of course. I wanted a big family anyway but I really was done at 4 kids. I had 2 girls and 2 boys it was perfect for us. So I'm in the mirror saying I'm going to show him and the test is ready. So I read the box again to make sure I'm reading it correctly and I understand it well. So I then look at the test and I look back at the box just to be certain.

I hold the test up to the box with the pictures saying PREGNANT to these line and NOT PREGNANT to this line. I then stop in dead tracks and I can't speak. I AM PREGNANT (looking dumb founded)! I just knew I would come out of the bathroom laughing in his face but I really couldn't talk. I open the door and I go out with the test in my hand. He's asking "so what does the test say"? I still couldn't talk at all because I really was shocked.

The kids are looking at me like mommy say something. I hand him the test and he busted out laughing and said your mom is having another baby. I was lost for words for a few days. I know how it happen but I was confused because we literally stop having unprotected sex for a while and I was pregnant for that while and had no clue. All I'm thinking about is the next big thing I can do so that I can help my man take care of this family of ours and just bust our butts. I always had a plan to open up a salon and I would set my own hours so that I didn't need a sitter for my kids they would be safe with me.

Now this is 2006 and in January 5, 2007 my baby boy was born. This was the last and hardest labor I endured. I went into labor with my little angel and man it was hard. I went in already knowing that I wanted an epidural because I cannot take pain. That's the first thing I asked for. So I had to wait for the anesthesiologist to come in.

    I thought that he was dealing with other women that was in labor and I said he has to hurry up. The contractions was coming so fast and I was scared to have a natural labor. No way was I going to do that and all the stories I heard. The anesthesiologist finally came in and introduced himself. I looked into his eyes and they were bloodshot red. What in the heck is wrong with this man?

    I thought either he was so tired from doing this all day or he had to just waken up. I barely could sit up right because the contractions was so on the second it felt like. My stepmother Sharon was there the whole time helping me. My man was at work and he was trying to get to me as soon as possible. I sat up and finally the meds was going in (so I thought). I had the best nurses with me helping me get through this pain.

All of a sudden I didn't feel any contractions I just started feeling really tired. I could tell that something was wrong because I was falling asleep but this just isn't normal from an epidural. I know I was very tired from being up and going through these contractions. The anesthesiologist placed the catheter but he put it in the wrong spot. Instead of it numbing me from my waist down it was going from my waist up. I was going out and I was saying help me but I didn't think anyone heard me.

Not knowing they can see all the monitors that was going off. My heart rate was dropping, my blood pressure was also. I heard the nurses ask me am I alright but I couldn't respond then I saw my nurse go into this room and the bag said crash kit. Then it was dark. The last thing

I heard was my step-mother ask what's wrong and is she alright. She called out my name and I wanted to talk but I just couldn't. I must had went completely out because I felt like someone just hit me really hard a few times and my nurse asking me can you hear me.

    Are you alright? I remember saying yes and then they said we turned the epidural off so that it can wear off. I then got really scared because I didn't want to have a natural birth. I had no choice they were waiting for my heart rate and my blood pressure to get back to normal. My nurse looked at me and said I'm not leaving your side until this baby is born. She was coming off of her shift but with everything that was going on she said she couldn't leave me until she knew that I was fine.

    I then saw the anesthesiologist standing by me. This dude almost killed me. My man then showed up and made it before the birth of our little man. I still had to do this natural. It was time the contractions was coming so fast I couldn't say anything just baring down like crazy. The doctor and my man was standing by my bed but I was so quiet (that's just me) they didn't know I was trying to tell them but I couldn't.

I couldn't grab out my hand because I was holding on to the bed ready to brake the arm rest or whatever it's called off. The doctor was telling my man what happen. She said something like we just have to wait until she looks like she's baring down and then she glances at me and I was staring at her. She said omg like how I think she is doing now. She quickly grabbed some gloves and said his head is out and they quickly broke down the bed to continue to deliver our son. I only pushed 3 times and yes it hurt but once he came out I felt no more pain at all.

It wasn't as bad as I thought having a natural birth but almost dying was not what I thought was going to happen to me. He was perfect and I was just fine. My nurse hugged me and said thank God and congratulated me and my man. That was the last time I saw her the whole time I was there. I was there for 3 days. I asked them can they take me in the back or right here tie my tubes.

I told them to take out anything they had to because I didn't want any more kids. I AM DONE!!! They told me that I had to come back to get it done. I didn't want that because of the feeling being put to sleep made me think that I was dying. I remember that when I had my 2nd child who was by a caesarean. I made that appointment before I went home though.

It was for February 14, 2007. I made that appointment and was there early. It was a in and out procedure. My cousin Tierra and her man Eric was there to help bring me home and make sure the kids and myself was good before leaving. Now we are a family of 7 man I felt an overwhelming blessing though because I was a kid growing up without my siblings that both of my parents had with other spouses. I was the only child between my parents and I wasn't raised with my siblings.

I was blessed because I can have my babies raised together with God's help and my man by myself. My baby was a momma's boy. He was stuck on my hip but the kids all spoiled him rotten. Love was all around me and now I had another blessing to share with Granddad. Seeing Granddad light up when we came to see him was all I needed to go through the week until we saw him again. I was a stay at home mom raising 5 kids, taking care of home and trying to hurry up and get my high school diploma.

I was determined to do this since I was hard headed as a teen just being difficult. My kids and I spent a lot of time with granddad even going to take him out from the facility.

He like his outings with us and we enjoyed it as well. Almost a year go by and things seem to start changing with my man and I. He said I was tripping but things just started changing up with his attitude. We stop talking at times, he would say some slick things out of his mouth and I wouldn't just let that happen again.

    I just was fed up. I am a strong woman and I wasn't going to let a man start disrespecting me and think I had to take it because I left my home to come with him or the fact that now I have 5 kids. Nothing isn't going to keep me feeling unhappy. I will pick up quick with my babies and roll out. I kind of figured it was coming to that but I really was hoping that it didn't. One night all the kids was in bed asleep and I was in bed watching television until I fell off to sleep. My man came in from somewhere. No we haven't been talking for a few days.

    So he came in and wanted to have sex. I'm thinking to myself (are you kidding me).

We are arguing and not talking but I'm supposed to give it up. I'm a very stubborn girl but so in this situation I wasn't giving in. So he told me well the apartment lease is up for renewing and he's not renewing it. So I'm in a situation where I don't have anywhere to go if he doesn't get his mind right.

I'm thinking look at what I got myself into just helping and being there for others like always. So a few days went by and I'm packing up my things trying to figure out my next step. The last day I knew I was trying to be stubborn but I wanted to have sex with my man. I did and when we finished he said to me "I still have time to renew the least so we can stay". That to me was saying if anytime you get into your feelings again and I don't do what you want then you can treat me anyway you want. It was a great that the kids just got out of school for summer break and my girls went with their father's mom like always every summer.

I told him "No I'm leaving because this shouldn't have happen like that. I told him that I need him to keep the boys that belong to him since I didn't have anywhere to stay myself and my oldest would stay with my father. The kids were gone the next day so I knew I had a couple of months to get something in order for my kids come back in a home. So, I called up my Aunt Rita and asked her can she help me. She picked me up the next day and took me to a property that she had in Baltimore. I didn't want to be there but I stay to myself anyway.

I called up the job I left because he wanted me to stay home so that put me where I felt I was starting all over once again from the ground up. Not having nothing but man all I ever did was help and want the best for my family and look where I let these men put me. Yes it was my fault to a point. I went back with hope instead of letting them show me my worth. I had to stay in this apartment but it was a place to lay my head. 1 bedroom a very tiny bathroom and a nice size kitchen but it had mice.

I would call every day to talk to my kids. He either would say he's not around them (he would be at work) but I needed to run it past him before I saw my boys, my babies (MY KIDS whom I was raising). I needed to check in with him and things seem to start turning far far left with this. Was he trying to put me in this situation so that I would lose the only thing I loved in this world and go completely nuts? I didn't like that because I never put anything on him like that. He could see them whenever he wanted when we weren't together.

So I decided to go and take my boys back and go hard with me caring for them myself. So one day I called him up and said that I wanted to take them out for ice cream and I would bring them back in a couple of hours.

He said that's fine and wanted to know the exact time. I laughed at him in my head lol but I had an agenda the whole time. Yes, they will be back at this time. My cousin picked me up and took me to where my babies were staying.

My youngest was only around 8 months and my other son was like 5yrs old. I pulled up to the house and they were sitting outside waiting on me with their sitter. I put my babies in the car with me and they never saw them again (well for a while). I took my babies up to my apartment and my oldest came back to. My old job wanted me to come back and I was back doing what I love taking care of the elderly. My Aunt also was the supervisor their but everything had to go through the man above. I had all the requirements and certifications to come back and get a raise.

My Aunt Rita told me that this apartment was temporary until something else came through. So like always I know I put myself in these situations by not waiting and obeying God. I thought that I could help him out just a tab bit that will never work out.

Always listen and feel what God has for you and just stand and things will get so clear.

Throughout all of this I had my family that was there for me and loved me and continued to say that I was a strong woman. Even though I knew and felt that I was just falling flat on my face by keep dealing with what I was. I was more upset with myself because I was looking into my children faces and even though they had smiles I just felt like I was failing them. I know I had to get strong for my babies and not worry about no one but my babies. So that's just what I did. I put my mind and soul into bettering things for my babies.

I got a call one day from my Aunt Rita that she had a place for my family. I was excited and when she told me where it was it was like another blessing. The exact same townhome I left when she didn't think it was a good idea was up for rent again. I left that home with 4 kids and was coming back in the house with 5 kids. I was getting back on my feet and it never felt so good but I kept in my mind that I'm 31 yrs. old.

What did I accomplish trying to be the best for others, giving these men kids that they wanted (I didn't mind having) and all I got was disrespect. I just kept telling myself with the help of my Aunt Nadine that I'm strong and many couldn't have kept going. I still smiled after it all and gave God the praise for bringing me through. So while back to work and had a sitter that I trust with my babies. I continued school and received my high school diploma and my babies was right by my side. Some family was there also and I appreciated them for being there.

I loved the fact that my kids can get back

to their rooms, I felt safe having family around me and I never heard (you should never had left in the first place). Through this all I still was going to see granddad but not as often as I was before. I was getting back on schedule for sure. I was struggling a bit because I was working paycheck to paycheck and trying to stay above water. Now I love freedom of having a home that's mine and all I ever wanted was a family to grow with and have a home to live in for the rest of our lives. I never thought that I….me, like why would I go through this type of stuff but this is life as we have to live it and make the best of it but never give up. God is great on all levels and he again gave me life and help me bless my babies with stability.

    I called up my cousin Tierra and we went looking at 2 houses and the second home was perfect for my babies and myself. So I moved in and life was so good. Of course I still had my kids' fathers still wanting the sex, saying they want my love (except my middle kid's father)…he just wanted sex. At this time I didn't want to be bothered by anyone but if I had an occasional date here and there I was content. I didn't act on them at all. I felt just to leave the past in the past and that is just where I left it.

Now we are in 2009 and I was a single woman with 5 kids but we are doing well and I'm so happy. I know that our future is great and it's starting here and now. It's pretty late for me and that is always on my mind but I won't let that stop me from keep going on and making a promising future for my babies. My dreams is so simple. It seems like the simple things was so far fetch but it wasn't something I knew I couldn't get eventually. I wanted a beautiful home, a truck that would fit my family very comfortable, bills paid with not living paycheck to paycheck and opening my own business (My Very Own Salon).

I was working toward it all and a tragedy

happen within our family.

A turn for the worst X2

I don't remember who contacted me but the family received a phone call that my granddad wasn't doing well and was rushed to the hospital. When I got there I was listening to what the doctors was saying to my Aunt's, my father and the family that granddad was having seizures back to back and he wasn't doing good. If you know our family all we do is pray. I'm not saying we are perfect but we know our God and prayer is what we know to do in great times, good times, bad times and bad situations. We pray for everyone even those whose blessing has come and we are thankful that they are happy. That's just the family we are.

We have ruff ones in here also but not one family in this universe is all put together (NOT ONE). One day while visiting my granddad I was in the room with my Aunt Felita and my little cousin that came to see granddad along with her mom. They talked for a bit and then left. So that left me alone with granddad for the first time since we all came to the hospital. Granddad was still unresponsive. The doctors said that granddad isn't responding to anything but whenever someone talked to him his forehead would wrinkle and his hand would move.

So I'm sitting in the room with granddad and I felt really stupid going up to him and talking to him when they said he couldn't hear us. I did it anyway. I pulled a chair up to the side of the bed and I told him that I love him. I didn't know what else to say at that time but I sang him a song. I have been trying to remember this song and I've been asking family forever. It goes like this "I love you, I love you, I love you lord today, Because you cared for me…in such a special way and yes we praise you, we lift you up and we magnify your name, that's why our hearts is filled with praise". I put granddad name into the song while singing it to him.

The point is that I had my one on one time with my granddad and I wanted to cherish him at that time. Before I left the hospital they were saying that granddad wasn't going to make it so they were giving everyone their time. I went home praying but I knew that I couldn't hold him here forever. I know that he wanted to be with God and in my heart grandma so I wouldn't be selfish. A few days pass and I wasn't going to see him because I didn't want my last vision of granddad doing bad and barely living. I received a call from my cousin Lisa telling me to come to the hospital to see granddad.

I told her how I was feeling and she said "No nique granddad is doing well." She said that he was up talking and he knew who she was. That made me feel good so I went to the hospital and walked slowly into his room. Granddad was in ICU but now they had him on another floor in a regular room because he just started getting well within days of us thinking we were going to say goodbye. I walked into the room and I saw Lisa sitting by granddad side of the bed. She looked so happy and that's when I felt relief in my heart.

 I pulled up a chair on the other side and we sat there talking a bit. Lisa was talking to granddad but his eyes was closed like he was sleep. She said he was tired so he was going back and forth sleep. She said he was talking to her so don't be afraid. So somehow we started talking about when we were young. Lisa said "Granddad, Nique was a bad little girl wasn't she". While his eyes was closed he said "No not Nique" and Lisa and I bust out laughing.

 Then granddad opened up his eyes and saw me. He looked at me and said with some excitement "Hey Nique" I was so happy and my heart was full of joy that he is sitting here talking with us and he knew who I was. I said "Heyyy granddad". The whole time Lisa was holding one hand (his left) and I was holding the other (his right).

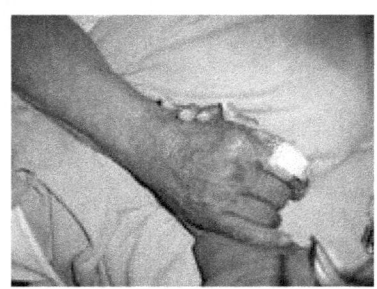

Lisa then said "granddad I wasn't bad was I"? Granddad waited a minute and said "sure you was". We laughed again and continued to talk quietly while still holding his hand sitting by his side. All of a sudden we heard him mumble something.

We asked him was he alright but he didn't respond. I asked Lisa what did he say and then we just was quiet to listen to see if he would say it again. All of a sudden he started again and I'm paying close attention and I looked at Lisa with my mouth wide open like Oh My Goodness. She said what's wrong. I said "when granddad was downstairs doing bad and we was in the room alone I held his hand and sung him a song." Lisa, granddad is humming that same song. He is telling me that he heard me when the doctors was saying different.

I was in shock and so blessed that he told me that he heard me and our conversation. God you are so awesome and I would cherish this moment for the rest of my life. I sat there a little longer but I was so hyped that he let me know that he heard me at that time. I know I told a few family members this story. I went home that night thanking God. A couple of days later they said granddad was doing good but he was being sent to hospice in Linthicum, Md.

He just couldn't stay at the hospital for a

long period and still needed to get well enough before he was sent back to the facility that grandma and granddad stayed. He wasn't there long when I got a call saying that granddad isn't doing well and they don't think he's going to make it through the day. I just couldn't imagine that because he was just up with Lisa and me talking. I didn't want to see this and the family was told to go right away to hospice facility. My sis Chanika was the first person I called when I got that phone call. I told her what they said and she told me that this was her dream last night.

    This was a day after my birthday Feb 20, 2009. She told me to call her anytime if I need her (she is always there for everyone). I took my time getting into my car and started driving down rt.100 towards Linthicum, MD. I said I didn't want to be the first one there so I pulled over on the side of the road and sat for about 20 min. I was going to make sure someone was going to be there when I got there. If they are saying he's not going to make it into the evening it really wasn't looking good then.

I would rather get the call that granddad is gone and grieve alone and go back home than to see him pass away in front of me. I couldn't see him like that. It was hard enough to go through being there with grandma and holding on to her body not wanting to let her go but my angels are leaving me and I couldn't bare to feel this feeling again. I talked to God and told him I just can't take it. Give me this strength that I need to go here and send angels before me. So I pulled off onto the road and headed to the facility.

I pulled into the parking lot and looked around to see if any cars looked familiar. I didn't notice any so I sat there for about 10min then thought someone maybe in there. I got out of my car and headed to the door still looking at every car. I got to the door and entered. The ladies was very nice and loving and the facility was beautiful inside. I told them I was here to see Mr. Jones.

They said no one was there but the family was called because she didn't think he was going to make it this long. She said it's any minute. I took a deep breath and she said "If you need us we are right here". I said thank you and she pointed out his room to me. I'm walking to the door and it was closed. I started opening it really slow because I didn't know what to expect to see. I was scared! The door was opening very slowly and I'm peaking around it and my eyes caught granddad eyes. He was looking at the door but I could tell right then it was a matter of minutes.

Thinking to myself someone better hurry up and get here with me. I walked in and said "Hey grandddad, he followed me with his eyes and I walked right up to his bed side. I had that feeling and my thoughts was to quickly call my cousin Michelle (Shelly) to let her know what's going on. I saw her in the hospital when granddad was doing a bit better and she said please keep her up to date on everything. I promised her I would. I told granddad I love him and I'm ready to call Shelly.

So I went into the bathroom and quietly told her that granddad isn't going to make it and I could really tell. She said "can I talk to him". I took the phone to granddad and at this time a couple of the nurses came in and adjusted him. He wasn't talking just breathing funny but still here with us. I walked to him and said "granddad Shelly wants to talk to you". I put the phone up to his ear because this conversation was between granddad and Shelly.

She talked to him for a few then I kind didn't hear anything so I put the phone to my ear. She said she was finished talking to him and she thanked me for calling. We said our "I love you" to one another and she hung up.

Both of the nurses was out of the room and I gave granddad my love. I talked to him and I thanked him for raising me to be the woman I am today. I said to granddad that I am so thankful for both of them and they are my angels.

I said "granddad please tell grandma that I love her and I miss her". I was watching his breathing and then I said to granddad "I love you" and he took his last breath……. The nurse walked and went to his bedside. I said while staring at granddad the whole time "He just took his last breath". The nurse said "No he's fine". I put some firmness in my voice and said "My granddad just took his last breath while I was staring at him, he's not breathing". She checked his pulse and looked at me with sadness and said I'm so sorry baby. I sat looking shocked, I looked around the room but no one was there with me.

I took two steps back and another nurse

came in and asked me am I alright. I said yes but I can't believe it. I didn't want to be here alone. I told them the whole story of me sitting on the side of the road just to avoid this here. They both said "He was waiting for you for a reason". They asked me to step of for a minute until they get him together so the others when they come he will be ready to come and see.

 I just sat for a minute staring at granddad face then tears started to fall. I walked out the room and I quickly called my cousin Ray Ray. I told him that I'm here alone and granddad just passed. We talked for a few and we hung up. Then I called my Aunt Rita and told her the same. The family was on their way but I seemed to be there at this time to give granddad my love and it was the time alone I needed and maybe he needed with me.

 I love my angels so much but one thing for sure is that no one ever know how much they meant to me. The nurses was finish and

I walked back in there with him and sat on the window seal for a bit and the door opened up. It was my cousin Tierra and her mom my Aunt Felita. We stayed in for a while then we left. I always said that if my parents ever left this earth I would move away far because they were what was keeping me, my backbone and I couldn't imagine living, looking at these visual memories where we all lived. I just couldn't pick up and leave but I really wanted to. If you understand and if I know my family they know how much I love them.

It was just that my grandparents, they were my parents all my life and they were there thick and then, and thicker and so much thinner. My everything was gone away from me forever.

This isn't a shot at my family at all but everyone had their own little family and my parents was gone from me to even look at. I drove away from that building crying my heart out but I knew that I needed something that I would cherish of them for the rest of my life. I called up my little brother Carl Jr and asked him to take me to his tattoo artist. Never thought that I would get a tattoo but this is what I needed for myself.

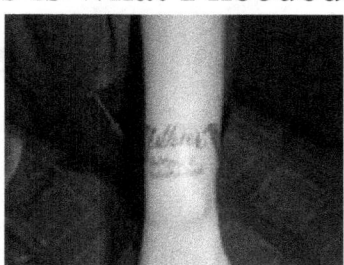

See my grandma passed away February 11, 2005 and was buried on my Aunt Evon birthday February 17, 2005. My birthday is on February 19 and granddad passed February 20, 2009 on my cousin Main Main birthday. It was now that I had to deal with yet another funeral and I didn't want to go. I hate them but I had to be there of course. That day came and I walked into this building and all the family was there. So so many came out.

    I walked down the aisle and there was granddad in his casket (that sounds hard to believe). I felt like I was the only one in the room and still was headed to the front to see him. I reached granddad and he looked just like him lying there. I started to cry and I walked away and found the first seat I could sit and it was next to my Aunt Sylvia. It was a beautiful home going for granddad and everyone spoke highly of him. That's all you could do really.

It was time to now pray and try to make it through this. God was there with me but I felt a peace upon me. I had my babies and I had my life so I just had to keep pushing and making things happen for my family. I was really starting to get up on my feet and I thought about moving out of state with my best friend Temeka B. I love that girl and never once have we had a falling out. For over 22yrs were nothing but true friends.

She actually was going to move me and my oldest when I had him to Florida in 1997 with her. I couldn't go and leave my grandparents. I seriously was thinking about it now. I even reached out to my kid's fathers and told them I'm leaving and we have to find a way that the kids could spend time with them. They were all for it then started switching up after a few days. Like now the kids was leaving with them for the summer except my oldest boy. He was going to either my father house or just stayed home with me.   He was gone though also a lot. The year of 2009 after my grandfather's passing in February that summer vacation my babies were all gone with their fathers and I was working my butt off.

The time my life changed forever

    I met this guy at my sisters' baby shower that I threw for her in the end of April or the beginning of May. My kids was gone for the weekend except my oldest boy. He help put up the decorations but ended leaving with my father for the weekend. At this baby shower this guy was telling my sister to hook him up. She said something to me but I just didn't want anyone at the time. I kind of did but then again

I wasn't looking forward to being hurt.

He was nice looking so throughout the day he was helping me do some things for the party, his mom was pushing the fact that he was interested in me and I had the thought … just maybe I'll entertain it (why not). When it was over they invited me over to a cookout they were headed to. I said I don't think I will make it because I had plans already with my cousin. They were leaving and everyone was saying goodbye and thank you for the baby shower. I was standing in the middle of my floor picking something up and he walked back into the house (the screen door was open) and asked for my number. I gave it to him and I turned to look out the window because he started to walk out the door and then he said he forgot something. Started walking towards me (I thought it was something behind me) I kind of moved to the side and he kissed me on my cheek. In my head I was like what in the hell he do that for and I frowned. He left out and said I hope you come by before you go out with your family then he left.

I locked the door, watched them pull of out of my sight. It was time that I get some me time. I took my shower, got dressed and rolled out to meet my cousin but she wasn't ready yet so I took a detour to check this dude out. I pulled up and got out of my car. I started walking towards him and everyone was out there (so much of his family). He asked me to come and say hello to everyone and I did. They invited me to stay but I said I already have plans.

So I said goodbye to everyone and he started walking me to my car. My cousin then came by and I got in the car with her not before he asked can he call me and I said sure. Now, from this point on we was started talking a lot on the phone, texting and many invites to his family functions. I accepted them but not once I knew none of his family. See while I was growing up as a teen I barely was around the area. Me and my crew Sweet T, Yogi, Big Kesha, Little Kesha and myself was always in another area chillin. Severna Park, Baltimore man you name it we always was gone.

I never met this family and even names wasn't familiar to me. My people knew them but I was lost. My kids left for the summer in June so I spent a lot of time around them. He was actually ready to move to another state but he said that he would stay here for love. It was a few months that we did everything together and we fell for one another. Now I wasn't going to let my past hurts get in the way so I would put my guard down so that I wouldn't mess up something here that could be great. I said I have to trust if I ever want love again and I did. I use to write all the time.

I would write about my hurts, pain and the fun times that I had. Writing helped me because it was my therapy and I didn't want to keep crying on my family. I was trying to heal myself with God pushing and guiding me to write. I had so many papers, books and had poems everywhere. I just love writing! It saved me really from having a break down. So I told this man this and he said that was a good idea and to continue to do this.

    The summer passed and my babies came back to me and was so happy. I loved these times because I always missed my babies while they were gone. We were getting ready for school coming back in so a lot of organizing was being done. Kids rooms was being moved around, new clothes were being hung up. I love changing around rooms and the kids knew once they come back they were ready. Not right away the kids knew about this guy because I was feeling him out around kids and he had a lot of kids around him far as family.

    He even took care of a few (meaning they were with him while family had to work). One day he invited me and my babies over to his mom home this was months after school had started. I thought this was a cool time to introduce him but we were only friends that wanted more but was taking our time. See I am the type that if I have an interest in you, you are the only one I am perusing. I can't say that's for everyone though. We took pictures and posted them on social media and so many of my friends was also his (mutual friends). They was saying that he was a good guy.

    These are people that I grew up with that thought they knew him well enough. He was good peoples I heard. So about October we became a couple. The kids like him and he was very interactive with them all and his nieces and nephews. The kids all took to one another also. It felt good and we did a lot together as a little family. We went out to eat, parks, like this guy took to my kids like they were his own (he didn't have any).

My little niece that was living with us he loved him some her. Auntie Nique and Uncle was always there for her. This man was the type that he drove everywhere unless he was dead tired but he drove us around. Going to the grocery store he pushed the cart, lifted the bags into the cart and getting to the car he put me in the car and he did everything else. When we would get to the house he took out the groceries out of the car and brought them into the house. He told me that I shouldn't have to lift a finger.

This is something that never changed the whole 3 years about that we were in it so far. He was the perfect gentleman and I didn't see any different. He sure knew what he was doing. I tell you this man came around my family, I stayed around his and we all was together often. I believe God was trying to tell me something and slow me down because I am a healthy woman. I look back at it now and think that I was so focused and into getting my cosmetology license I didn't think or even got a feeling that anything was going on. Since I was communicating with my kids about being careful and sticking with one another getting home from school just make sure you are there for one another.

I knew I had a great man on my side that cared for my kids so I had no worries. One day my man, my daughter and myself were sitting in my room watching television and I was on the computer. I felt very faint and nauseous. I just didn't understand why I couldn't get up to move even though my mind was thinking it, my body wasn't cooperating. I was determined to move so I pushed up with all my might thought I better lay down but when I tried to turn to get up I couldn't move. I was sitting there looking at my bed like (just get up).

I tried to say "something is wrong with me" and all that came out was nothing but mumbling. That scared me! I was standing for a second then I started to fall so my boyfriend jumped across the bed and grabbed me before I hit the ground. My daughter was there and got really scared. He told her to leave the room quickly. He ask me what's wrong but I couldn't talk and my whole left side was numb, I couldn't see clearly, my heart was racing out of my chest. He couldn't understand me when I was trying to talk to him.

He called 911 right away and when I heard him say "she's trying to talk but I can't understand anything she's saying, she can't stand alone I'm holding her up now. They were on their way and I just thought I was dying. I was rushed to the hospital (I had a stroke). The doctors said that it could be stress and so many other people says that you could be stressing and not know it. I think that could have been it but my father and all my family came to the hospital and he did what he would do. He took my kids to his house until I got better and I'm so thankful for him doing that.

    He didn't think one time. My step-mother (Sharon) and sisters (Lashawna & Tyesha) were also a huge help and I appreciate them for that. I'm not sure who else was helping out with my kids but I thank everyone for helping out. I sat in the hospital with my man on my side all day and night for a week but not getting better. Well, I had to walk slowly to the bathroom but the moment I took a couple of steps the nurse would rush in to see if I was alright. I didn't understand why but she said that my heart rate was so high they thought I was ready to die (yes, but in their own words).

    One day I had so many family and friends come to see me and the doctor comes in with his results. So he said that on my MRI Scan they saw a few spots on my brain and it's MS (Multiple Sclerosis). Man I am one that doesn't like crying because it makes me feel weak. I said they're going to take more test but I still couldn't stand much by myself. I broke down in front of my family because I wasn't ready to leave them and my babies of course but still I believe in GOD and I knew I was going to be healed. My best friend Ashley was coming in to see me but got sick and when she came into my room in a wheel chair I laughed.

What was going on with her I thought? She came to see me and ended up being admitted needing a blood transfusion. Iron level was low so I had her to visit with in here also. I was in this hospital for 5 days and I told my father I need to get out of here and go to John Hopkins in Baltimore, Md. The very next morning I was discharged and not walking and everything my father put me in his car. I was so dizzy I couldn't sit up or open my eyes. I laid in the back seat the whole ride feeling awful.

So I know I had prayers rolling in. I was praying also but God was there the whole time.

I was admitted in John Hopkins and they did test after test. They had me trying to stand and walk and minute after minute I was getting better. Now my talk was getting better, I could hear myself and I sound better. I ask my boyfriend who was by my side the whole entire time and my father can they understand me and they said yes.

I wasn't 100% but I will take this here getting better. I started walking alone and getting a little better. They did another MRI and absolutely nothing on it. I was in this one machine for about 1 ½ hours and I came out with a great news. The doctors came in the next day and said yes, I had a stroke but with me improving so well quickly I could go home soon. That sound so great to me and all I did was look up and say thank you GOD and grandma & granddad thanks for your prayers.

I was released to go home I believe the next day or that day after. I was back home with my babies.

The day I died mentally

In the year 2011 the month of February after my birthday was a day that I never thought I would ever see. We were all home the kids, my man and myself. We was all watching television in my room. My man was getting ready to go to work. It was over night and we kind of was arguing a bit a few days before. The arguments was getting to where I really wanted quits and I was going to do just that but waiting for the right time that my babies wasn't going to be around.

I have been going through some things with him but we were working them out. We talked marriage but it was normal to have situations but the test was to see if we could work through them. So he went to work and the kids and I was still in my room watching a movie until it was bed time. My youngest daughter stood up and said that she had something to tell me. I turned and looked at her but something in me was nervous but I told the other kids to leave the room quickly so I could talk to her. She was 10 at this time because she just had a birthday a couple months before. So, she discussed with me some young girl problems that was normal for a young girl.

So I told her that I would take her to the doctors the next day so don't worry. She then insisted that I was to check her out myself and she is the type that don't let anyone see her but she knows that mommy makes sure that my girls are straight because we talk about those girl things. So when she insisted that I look to see if she was alright. My heart started pounding so hard. Something told me to ask her and my heart was full of fear. I looked at my baby girl that I've been protecting all of these years from horrible people in the world and my question to here was "did someone touch you in a bad way"? I was so afraid of her answer but I wanted it to be the right answer but when she took both of her hands and covered her mouth in fear and said I'm scared.

My breath was gone…it was hard for me to catch a breath to ask her again and I did. "Did somebody touch you in a bad way"? I told her that she's safe with me and she can tell me anything. While I'm talking to her so much is running through my mind. I asked her who touched her and she said his name. She stated that it was my boyfriend at the time but when she first said his name my mind was so gone the moment she said someone touched her. So when she said his name I said "who is that"?

She then pointed to where he was standing before he left for work not long ago. My first words was "I'm going to kill him". She said in fear "No mom that's why I didn't tell you right away because I knew you would want to hurt him and I didn't want him to hurt you". I grabbed her close and we cried for a minute and I said to her "ok, I'm not going to do anything". I told her she will never have to worry about seeing him again and In my mind I was saying so much more and I was plotting some things in my head to do to him. I called my bestfriend Shakia because she was always there for me good or bad. Awesome and a beautiful person inside and out.

    She was in shock and I was so confused to what I was suppose to do at this point. I didn't want to call the police until his body was laying at my foot. So I called my Aunt and the only words from me was I need you here now.

    This isn't something I would ever just call and say. Her words to me was "I'm on my way". On her way she stopped and picked up another one of my Aunt's and they were on their way to us. I didn't know what to do. I was trying to hold it together until my Aunts got to me. They were there in a heartbeat but it felt like forever.

They put my other kids in another room and told them that they need to talk to my daughter and myself but we are right across the hall. So we went into the room and I told my daughter to tell them what he did to her. This man was a 35 year old but desired a 9 year old baby. I called 911 right away with my baby girl standing by my side. My Aunt's left us in the room to talk with 911 and as soon as I said my daughter just told me that my boyfriend molested her I broke down and started crying & hyperventilating.

I couldn't talk but I was trying to, I was crying way to hard and I couldn't pull myself together. I heard the dispatcher telling me to take a deep breath and my daughter grabbed me so tight and said "mom calm down it's going to be alright" I cried harder. I should've been the one saying this to her, well really I should have protected her more. I did everything that a crazed scary mom would do and say to make sure my kids was careful of people like that. They could never go outside alone, they couldn't go around the corner because I couldn't see them in my eyesight. If one wanted to come in the house they all had to walk that one home and then they can go back out front.

I was always on top of it but in my home this had happen to my baby and I never saw signs of this. Now, I always asked all of my kids because they were not in my eyesight all of the time. I have asked all of them have anyone ever touched them in a bad way. Actually, I asked my daughters about 3 days prior to her coming to me and telling me this. I pulled them in their room, shut the door and talked to them and said if anyone tried you make sure you tell me right away. Now the craziest thing about this all is.

I was in cosmetology school passing all my test just feeling great about accomplishing one of my goals and for about 2 weeks my body wasn't letting me get up to go to class. I mean I never missed a day but for these 2 weeks every night I was having dreams and nightmares that someone was being molested. The fear was so strong it was in my gut and I would wake up scared to death and telling him that someone close to me in my family was being molested. He would hold me and tell me that's it's alright but this dream would happen every single night. At this time it wasn't happening because my daughter told the cps and the police the time it happen to her. So when the police came to my home I told him what was going on and my daughter was sitting there.

The officer first said "First I want to tell you how proud of you I am! So many kids don't tell their parents but you did and I'm so proud of you." The officer said that if he was to come back to the house its best that we don't be there. I already told the cop my plans and he said "Believe me I understand but you did the best thing so let us handle it". So I packed my kids up and left that night. We went through the procedures of a child being molested. The hospital visit, cps called to interview, the whole 9.

 A few hours came and I kept getting phone calls from him. I wouldn't answer of course but he was at my house wondering where we were. He couldn't get in because we jammed the locks. When he left a voicemail on my phone saying that he was at the house I called the police and they went to the house quickly. One of the officers was on the line with me but my boyfriend didn't know. I told the officer where I had to take my daughter and why they told him to leave the house now and don't come back.

He was going to get called in for questioning anyway so that's the reason I'm assuming they didn't take him right away. While sitting here waiting for the doctors to do all of these things to my daughter because of him and my phone was going off so much from his calls and voicemails. One of the messages was saying that "she is going to be fine and he's praying for her". No one told him anything so why would he say that. I told the cps everything that he was saying to me on my voicemail. They told me to just keep them and I did.

A few days later I took my kids to school, my Aunt was with me to go check my house out. We walked up to the door and it was kicked in. It was a very large picture of us above my bed. He took that picture and ripped it in small pieces and placed it on the floor in my room. Throughout the time that my daughter was going through this everyday all day long he would leave voicemails, apologizing but wouldn't say why. Then he would say he miss me and love me so much, then he would cry on there.

It was so much and I would contact the cps and the officer that was on the case letting them know everything he was saying. It was awful and I had to tell her father this and at the same time keep calm as possible but that was gone after I left the hospital with my baby girl. My mind started to go quickly. I couldn't talk to anyone because I would break down and cry, scream and blame myself for trusting another man.

See it doesn't matter if you know these people or not anyone can be a pedophile and lurk until he/she see the timing is right for them.

The cps and detective got together and took care of my daughter and I. Right away they set us up for therapy. Not before they talked to my other kids because they were in the house also. They had to go to my kid's school and talk to them. Nothing happen to them so they put their focus on my daughter and since I was gone mentally (my mind) they had to get me help right away. Now, they contacted him and this time his family didn't know what was going on but he knew because the detective contacted him before and he kept that hush hush from them.

    He knew what he was being accused of but still not one person in his family knew because he wouldn't say anything. If someone accused me of something so horrific I would try to clear my name, I would tell my family for support (anything) my family would know. He did not tell one soul but he was in contact with the police because they let me know everything that they were doing and what was going on. I received a call from both detective and cps and they said that they called him to come down to take a "voice analyst test". I asked her was that a lie detector test. She told me no it's to listen to your tone of your voice while being ask questions and it will pick up if you get nervous basically.

I said give him a lie detector test but they said this was enough. I was pissed with them! So I just waited for the call back and the results. That call came in and I felt this was going to be stupid. Now everyone that knows him (he talks real calm) he can control his voice and himself very easy. I saw it for myself getting into it with others or if someone he thought was trying to talk to me. He was great at that so I was really pissed when they said he pass but still it wasn't a lie detector test.

Now they are saying that they believe my daughter but to take it to trial they don't want to do that because ….LISTEN TO THIS…. because it would be hard to prove to the jury. Just because it was a full house and how could it happen. Are you kidding me? I told them I want them to take this to trial and if they want to put me on the stand for any reason do so. I know I really didn't want my baby girl have to get up there and see this piece of shit. I didn't want to see him myself but if this would save someone else child I would do it. They didn't go any further with the case and they let this bastard go. I was so hurt and knowing what I was going through I couldn't imagine what my baby girl was going through mentally holding all that in.

My daughter and I was set up for therapy starting in March of 2011 the same day but with different therapist of course. I never asked my baby girl how it went in her session. I waited for her to want to talk about it to me. She talked to me every day about how if she didn't want to talk about it they would just play a game. Whenever she was ready they would and she started getting comfortable with her therapist and it was great for her. It was a few times I would be in my room with the door closed because all I did was cry.

She would knock on my door and I would get myself together and say come in. She just would say "Mom, can I cry?" I would say of course baby. Shut the door and she would come to me and she would cry and I would hold her and cry myself and tell her that we are going to get through this together. I was trying to stay strong but I was falling further and further in depression. Every week was the same old thing going to therapy and for me I couldn't talk about it. Brining up his name in the session would make me very upset.

My therapist was really concerned as she stated many of times and she would try to get me to do different exercises. She would ask me something and I would use different things to express my answer. I not knowing I would go into therapy and I would wear heavy clothing, a hood and my body language was very shut

in, closed, like my arms stayed cross over my chest, my legs stayed crossed, I kept a hood on and she had plenty of napkins for me. I was so lost for this whole year I did nothing but isolate myself because I couldn't be around anyone.
I did nothing but stay in my room. See what I knew that he did to my baby all I ever saw was the visual in my head.

    I tried hard thinking of anything else but I would be in my room and looking at my wall it was playing out in my head, I just would be sitting and it just kept coming across my mind and nothing but tears would fall. I wasn't any good to anyone. My kids was home but I'm so proud of my kids for being there for each other. My oldest took over cooking for the kids. They all made sure everyone took care of their hygiene. They came together and they just knew mommy wasn't feeling well.

    They always came in asking me am I alright. I would play hard but as soon as the door shut my face was drowning in tears. I thought this therapist was supposed to help me but all she keep doing is talking about the situation that happen. How was that helping me? My mind was so gone the whole entire time where I forgot to pay my bills like I couldn't remember to do anything. My therapist said that they would have to get me someone like a personal assistant to help me.

I was losing it and I couldn't see it getting any better. Like I really never thought in my life would I have to hear that so close to my family (molestation) and in my own home.

My baby girl was getting better and her dad was coming around and one thing for sure was she wanted him close to her and I opened that up. It made her feel safe and I was hoping it would help me also with getting out of this feeling. We left our home for about 4 months because I was in fear. I was petrified to be there where it happened also.

My Aunt Felita (Aunt Baby my son calls her) and Uncle James opened up their home and insisted us to stay with them as long as I wanted. The kids loved that. They were great for being there for us and I Thank them, love them and appreciate them both for it!

He started coming over with me so I wouldn't be alone while the kids was in school for the day. If no one was there with me all I did was stand at my bay window peaking out. I would walk back and forth from my door to my window and never could get any rest. He came back y'all and he said all the right things again but I knew this would be different because of the situation we all was put in and we all can you know heal together. She was happy and that made me feel better and start to get out of the house a little (to the porch) and get some fresh air. I was a mess.

Well it's so crazy because that good feeling was so quickly gone because this man just can't get his self together (what kept us broken up was the cheating). I just had to put my focus on getting better alone and push but all my pushing wasn't pushing. It was more me falling down a road I didn't know how to get out of. Going into 2012 should have been trying to get my mind right but I just couldn't no matter what and I tried very hard. I was going to every single therapy session even when I didn't want to be there. I was just so tired of being here in this life and I couldn't function at all.

    I was just so tired because no matter the time of the day or the moment I just keep seeing all the details that was told to me that this disgusting thing did to my baby girl. It just came to a point that I wasn't thinking at all and I was DONE with life. This day I had to go to my last therapy session and I wasn't going to go but I had too. I was in a really bad place and I cried all day. You may be thinking (all I heard her keep saying is she's been crying) but that's the truth. My baby was violated in a horrible way and she shouldn't have been exposed to what he did to my baby.

I had everything going through my mind. I just couldn't take it anymore. On the way to therapy I had to travel across a bridge. Now I will tell you since the beginning when my daughter told me what happen to her no once did I pray. I said my mind was gone and I forgot to even think about GOD. That's just so horrible to say and to think of but it's the honest truth. God just knew that I wanted to die and I was so ready to stop feeling this pain for my baby and myself. I just knew I was ready to end the hurt and pain.

I contact my cousin Tierra and wrote a long text telling her that I love everyone and tell my kids I love them so much. I told her I was so broken I couldn't get out of it and this was my way to do so. I then turned off my phone so I wouldn't get any distractions.

So I'm headed to this bridge and I'm driving pretty fast. My plan was to go fast enough and at a certain point to turn my wheel so that I would go over the bridge. So this was it! I started driving fast and my mind said….go and I grabbed my wheel and went to turn it hard but it didn't budge.

    I just kept going straight. My wheel locked up on me and I couldn't turn it. Just as quick my mind went right off of that and I kept going to therapy. My face is wet with tears barely able to see but I reach my therapy session. I sat in the car for about 5 minutes before actually going in because I couldn't stop crying. I decided to go on in and the moment my therapist saw me we walked into the room, shut the door, turned to me and she said I'm so afraid right now. She grabbed ahold of me and I broke even more. She held me a way God would have done if he was here in the flesh.

    I can't tell you exactly what she said but

she have told me that it wasn't fair how things went with us within the system. She have saw this often and it's not fair for the families going through these horrific times. I left my last session with remembering a lot of things she said and showed me how to breathe in hard times, to do certain exercises to keep calm and she said to stay in contact with friends and family and stop isolating myself. I told her I just couldn't. She gave me a lot and it got soaked in but I had to try and put it to the test but at this time nothing was going good for me. I decided to go and visit my grandparent's grave which I never did since when they were laid to rest.

It's so hard to see this but today I did and talked and cried to them. This was my goodbye……

I then left them and still felt so bad walking away and they aren't by my side. This is what hurts so bad but I walk away looking back until I reach my car and blow my last kiss to my angels.

I am heading home and still thinking I just can't do this thing called life. I pull up in front of my home and I sit in my car and I'm crying so hard I can barely breathe. I don't remember why I turned on my phone but I called up my Aunt Nadine and told her how I felt. She was always one that gave me her advice but it was coming from God and still till this point I did not pray or talk to GOD. My Aunt always tells It like it is but the family knows that she's speaking for our best interest. She will not lie to or have you thinking one way.

It's always nothing but the truth and that's why I love her so much. She told me that I was being selfish but to be honest I didn't see that or feel that. I didn't get what she was trying to say because I still was pretty much gone. After being on the line with her when we hung up I wanted this thing to be over like right then. I remember a huge tree stump around where I lived. I thought to drive so fast into it and I will be done with this thing I was living called life. I turned off my phone.

My kids was gone and I was home alone.

So I turned on my car started driving then it was that time to just floor the pedal. I pushed my foot to the floor when I saw this huge tree stump. When I pushed my foot on the accelerator my car didn't go anywhere. It just started jerking really bad with no speed and I was like (dang I can't even kill myself right). I turned around and headed back to my home. Now my car drove back home just fine with no hesitation.

I got out the car, went into my house, locked my door and went into my room. Crying still I saw these pills and grabbed them and took one and ready to take another and couldn't swallow the first one. I actually was going to take one by one until the bottle was gone. I just couldn't get them down so all of a sudden a loud scream came out of my mouth and I yelled. No words and what came out of my mouth next was a shock to me. I screamed and the word JESUS came out and I just held it for the longest time. I think that I held this scream for a good 5 minutes and At that moment I felt something change within me that I can't explain.

From that moment I honestly felt strong and I got stronger and stronger by the minute. I thought about it and I ask God for forgiveness because not once the whole time I called on God, not one prayer, just nothing because my mind was gone. The next day my kids came home and I just held them and they felt that mom was feeling better. I made sure that I prayed every minute I could. I didn't ever want to forget about prayer but I talked to God and I know he understood.

A couple of weeks went by and I was laying in bed late night and I saw a Facebook friend of mine posting about something that caught my eye.

He was all pumped up and I wanted to know what was going on with what he was talking about. I told him to call me and he did. We talked on the phone and all he kept saying was come to one of his events. With all that said he introduced me into the MLM world. Mr. Coates (Guy) Being an entrepreneur and stating to me that being home with my kids while making money was right up my alley. I was afraid of leaving my kids so this was what I needed to happen for me.

 We talked so much about it and God placed things right into place so that I could start my very first home based business. This had all my time and energy so it kept my mind off of all the bad things my family went through and I was focusing on my family future. I talked to him and and just 2 weeks prior to me seeing his post on social media I just tried to take my life 3 times. This is a blessing in itself. So the next year 2013 I met some great people within this company that I look up to and I see their passion for helping many and accomplishments and I'm so proud of them. They all played a key role in my development and I thank you! My mind was so busy on a bright future because your passion was felt through everything you do. I thank you! Just to name a few because they really help me heal and they don't even know.

    Mr. Aaron Burt, Mr. Demarco Lucus, Mrs. Danielle Ikpe (Strand), Mr. Joseph Butler, Mr. Cody Mackie, Mr. Justin Tayor. You all helped change my way of thinking and me getting back to who I am In Spite of all I've been through. Thank you from the bottom of my heart!

A new beginning and knowing my worth

    Things started to look promising for me personally and mentally. This company I was with is what grew me and made me even more a stronger woman. It was no way that I wanted to work for someone else, make them money, work their schedule and leave my kids. I fell in love with being an entrepreneur working for myself. All my time was being home when my baby's got up for school, watching them get on the bus and being there when they get off the bus. I also added to my home base business having a hair boutique and this would take me traveling.

I couldn't wait until this also was bringing in money for my family. I was on the right track for what I loved being apart of.

In October of 2013 my son Daeshaun and I was sitting at Chick-Fil-A drive through food restaurant waiting to order. It was two cars in front of us. The car directly in front of us was next in line to order and she got out of the car and went to the back door doing something. I said out of my mouth to my son "She better get back in that car, that's dangerous". So she did and she moved up and ordered. Now it was our turn and I saw a car pulling up behind me but I was ready to order and all of a sudden BANG and a very loud scream, we were hit from behind.

The car behind us hit us. I didn't know what was happening but I knew my car was moving really fast and I couldn't stop it with my foot pushing the break to the floor. My son and I was hit so hard we was pushed a good 10 feet and I hit the car in front of me and pushed her about that much. I was dazed and so confused but I wanted to get out to see what just happened. I saw the lady in front of me get out and quickly go to her back seat. She picked up an infant to see if he was alright and then came to us.

I opened my door but I couldn't stand right away. My whole body was shaking so bad I just sat there trying to get myself together but I was so worried about everyone. My son Daeshaun was just fine. He made a joke like "It felt like we were in tunnel vision in a xbox3 game". I told him he was crazy but he was fine. We were just a little shaking up. I had to think about what just happen and I know I heard a scream so I asked my son was I screaming.

He laughed at me and said no someone behind us was screaming. It was an old couple and the man was driving. He said something happen and his foot just dropped off of the break and hit the gas. This man was 92 years old and his wife. I felt so bad for them and she was really shaking. They weren't hurt. No one was hurt thank God for that. My car was totalled but everyone walked away fine.

I lost my only transportation and still have to pay until the car is paid off. All I know is a blessing is coming and I was just to wait. Let me tell you how I was disappointed but the blessing came because I was hit from the back by another car so my son and I was paid for it (it help me pay up on my bills some). Just what we needed some extra money and I saw the blessing in it. I just didn't know about a week later something else is going to come up in my life. I was sitting in my room watching television and it kept seeming like this same dang on commercial kept playing over and over.

    I thought this is crazy and what if it was for me. Had me paranoid like crazy. You know how you keep seeing something and you wonder are they talking to you? It was a cancer commercial and never would I ever have done this but my hand went down to my right breast. This is so crazy but the moment I touched my breast there was a lump the size of a apple and I gripped it. My hand held this lump and it was very hard. My eyebrows went up like (what the hell). I then let it go and just laid there.

    I know my first thought would I need to get this checked out right away. No, not me! I ignored it because I didn't want no doctor tell me that I have cancer. No I can't hear those words and if it is that I don't want to know.

Just let me go on to glory. Everyday I would grab it and it was still there.

This lump was big and not going down but why didn't I feel it before. How did something so huge get there and I not feel it in the shower everyday? I ended up telling my girls grandmother and she was on me. I thought I shouldn't have told her because I don't want to worry her if it was cancer. She put it to me like this…"You better call and make an appointment by the morning! I will be calling you early and if you don't I'm going to give you hell until you do".

She made me promise her and I do keep my promises. So I promised her I would but I really didn't want to call. Well, I called the next morning and made an appointment with my doctor. Yes, she called right when I hung up with the doctors office. She was the one that made me do this and I thank her and appreciate her for it. Thank you Mrs. Pam!! The day came and my doctor did an exam and right away he felt it.

He sent me to a specialist and they had to do a sonogram first and they saw it but didn't know what it was. They wanted to be sure but it was a huge lump. They then moved around and there was another behind the big one. They then did a biopsy to test it where they also placed a tiny clamp in my breast and a mammogram was done. This was done in case it was cancer and they had to surgery, they would go to the right place. So I went home and called her to let her know what was going on.

I kept her up on this situation. She had prayers going all over for me. A couple of days went by and I was talking on the phone with my cousin Tierra and I received the call from the doctor office. I already knew what they were going to say because they called me instead of asking me to come into the office. Well on this call she stated that the lump they found was in fact CANCER. I couldn't hear anything else after that. Like I'm not sure what the heck she was saying but she was talking. When we hung up I had to call back to understand what she just said to me.

So they gave me instructions on the next steps to take but I had to go and have surgery to remove them. They called me to schedule this and I was there ready to get this out of me. My family was there with me but I always said "I'm fine" when really my mind was saying again I can not get a break. I started thinking "Why am I here on this earth" like really. At this time didn't know my purpose and I know it wasn't just to bring kids into this world and for me to just die off. I started getting really confused and this was coming to a breaking point.

When will I see my goals, my husband, my happy family in our home and taking family trips? I'm just not understanding my life right now.

I went into surgery and they remove it. I am in pain for about 3 weeks but I had pain pills and I wanted to make sure I wasn't feeling it all. I get a call from the doctor to tell me that they didn't get it all and it was bigger than they thought. So I had to come in for surgery again. I made that appointment to get put to sleep once more (which I hated). They then took a wider margin out of my breast to make sure they got all the cancer this time. I went home and later on in the week got a call that "I AM CANCER FREE".

My kids knew because this I wasn't going to hide it from them. They will see me go through the struggles but look at mommy being strong. They just didn't know inside I was dying. I Had to get myself back on track and not let this get to me. So I started putting so much of me into my business which I was trying to get rolling in for my family. Dealing with that in 2013 and now we are in the new year and nothing but putting all my past behind me because prayer works and help heal me mentally.

    Nothing else could do this and I made sure this would be done because I love my God and all of this I've been through and going through is for a reason. I'm not really sure now but I know it's for a reason. On March 7th, 2014 I went to the A lol Atlanta with 2 of my cousins Tierra and Sheneea on a business trip. We were so exited because things seemed so clear for us all and we were happy about our furture for our families. We was going for the weekend and due to come back Sunday. We met a few of the ladies that we was in business with whome we bonded with through the internet. My boo Deja and Morgan we met more great people there also. These girls are just the best and I love my chicks.

    We all have been through trials but it's great when you have someone that listen and pray with you to get you through and these girls were doing just that. Our other partner was suppose to be there but she couldn't my other boo/sis Domanice. We missed you hunny! It went great the event the time spending with my cousins but missing my crew so much (my babies). I made sure they were safe before I left of course. I felt great on the way there and we spent some time with Deja that night.

    That Saturday my stomach was upset and I felt a little dizzy, just not feeling well really. Saturday around noon we walked to get something to eat at Gladys Knight chicken and waffles before our event and after I started feeling a little worst but was able to move around. I didn't feel like it really but I pushed myself to be. I was out quickly after our ride back to the Hotel I was in bad shape and wanted to lay down. My cousins later on that night went to get a snack but I stayed in the bed thinking it was the change in the weather that had me getting sick. The next morning we got up because it was time to go home.

Man I felt bad and it wasn't going away. I then thought maybe it was the food from the night before.

Getting back home I gave my babies love but fell in the bed right away. I was in my bed for 2 weeks not eating, only getting up to shower and go to the restroom. Getting up was a hassle because I couldn't walk independently. I was either leaning on my kids to get to the bathroom and the back to bed. I had no appetite and just a couple of steps I would be out of breath, heart pounding out of my chest. It was bad but still I was trying to diagnose myself now.

Maybe I have the flu (I never had the flu but assumed) but 2 weeks went by and I just couldn't take it anymore. I was just laying in bed now and my heart was racing so fast. My symptoms now was

~Rapid heart rate w palpitations

~Extreme tiredness

~Difficulty breathing

~Frequent urination

~Difficulty sleeping

~Muscle ache (my whole body)

~Excessive sweating

~Shakiness

So I called my father and asked him when he get's a chance can he take me to the hospital.

I never had the flu so the symptoms I didn't know. I went to the local hospital to be seen about the flu. They said "your heart is racing and your blood pressure is high. When they said that I told my father "they are crazy and I'm getting out of here and go to John Hopkins". This hospital wanted to send me home with meds to slow my heart rate down but they didn't try to admit me.

So the next day I went to John Hopkins in Baltimore, MD. Right away they hooked me up to be moniter and saw that my heart was racing so fast but I only was laying there dozing of. My heart rate was 160bpm (normal is from 60-110 the most). They came in and said we are admitting you. So my father and stepmother Sharon (I know they were tired) waited a while before they left. We all was dozing off and laughing at one another catching each other.

I had a team of about 7 doctors trying to figure out why wouldn't my heart slow down and blood pressure wouldn't go down. So they have me in the hospital for 5 days and they are taking so many test. I felt so bad and all I could do was just lay there. My father, stepmom Sharon and 2 sisters Lashawna and Tyesha came to visit me there and they brought my favorite food (Chipotle) I loveeeee me some of that! So the 3rd day the doctors came in and said ok we think we found out and we are going to start you on some meds. My T3 and T4 levels were very high…It was my thyroid in the front of my throat.

It was working really hard. Those were my symptoms then later on they took my weight and I had lost about 15lbs since March 8th until I was admitted. I was shocked and excited because this weight I was trying to lose anyway (do you know I've been trying to get back to 150lbs). With all the test they took I knew nothing else was going on. They took test for everything from my blood and everything was fine. They tried me on a medication to see how I would react to it.

It eventualy work for me but I had to follow up with a specialist dealing with Thyroid (endocrinologist). They call this Hyperthyroidism (Graves Disease). Now I'm a woman that lived through rape, sexual abuse, mental abuse, physical abuse, cancer and I'm still living with

Graves Disease but I'm living only because of God. I am on medication everyday for the rest of my life for this (that's what the doctor said). Sharing my life with so many is something I always thought I wanted to do but my story wasn't ready back then. I thank God for my life because I am a very strong woman. I do have my days but I look back and reflect on where I was and now where I am and where I am going to be.

God didn't let me take my life or let anyone else end it for a reason. So I won't let anyone stop me. Why in my young age (wink wink) did I all of a sudden start getting sick out of the blue. God had a plan for me and he saw in me the strong woman that he made. He also saw that I now understood my purpose on this earth. I am blessed to share my testimony with many. So I say to you I WAS HER CRY, I WAS HER PAIN NOW I AM HER LAUGHTER , HER JOY THROUGH THE RAIN. I

AM LIVING AND I ONLY CAN BE HER DOMINIQUE DANYELL JONES

I am a woman with trials & hurdles but now I'm wiser (far from perfect) but I know my worth. I'm a mother of 5 wonderful blessings that I have to live for (God's blessing he shared with me). I live for my babies and many others out here to be a part of your life and let God use me to help or maybe guide you. IT'S STRENGTH IN YOUR VOICE, IT IS GUIDANCE IN OUR HEART, IT'S VISION IN YOUR SOUL BUT IT'S POWER IN THE NAME OF JESUS!!!!! Use him, talk to him, and let him guide you.

You may think you need a movement right now but God already made your steps in life. Find that first step and just get back on course.

At the end of it all I smile and I'm happy because and only because GOD loves my family with myself and I trust him with everything. My life was a rollercoaster ride and all of it was a lot of learning experiences that I had to learn the hard way. You can't love someone that has problems and don't want to change, you can't change someone no matter how perfect you think you are for them. They are their own person and what they feel is totally different than your feelings. Don't listen to everything! You have to see it and let them prove it man or woman.

Yes I have 5 kids and I love them all equally. Yes my kids have 3 different fathers because 1st we fell in love, 2nd they all didn't have kids and wanted me to be the mother (that says a lot for me), and 3rd no matter what I will not let a man take me through hell and stay with him long term and let this be my life. I was in long term relationships with these men before I moved on but I let myself continue the time I did with these men. Time went on and I knew what was best and removed myself instead of continuing to cry, be depressed and ran over. All in all I wanted different and I knew God was going to give it to me and my babies instead of me looking for myself.

I made mistakes also and I'm not perfect but all I wanted again basically is love and stability. Don't ever get a cold heart and not let the word "LOVE" define your presence. LOVE is many things but it doesn't supposed to hurt. So if someone tells you that they love you but continue to hurt you "GET AWAY" and don't turn around until you "SEE" change. In all that you do trust in GOD and he will see you through.

Thanking all that touched my life in a positive way

I want to give thanks to my God who never left me when mentally I passed on. You were there through it all but gave me what I needed from the beginning. You are my everything and I love you infinity!

To my family and friends and you all know who you are. I want to thank you all for being a part of my life and you may not know what you did to help me but you were all very much my backbone. If I wrote why you all were there for me that would be more than another book. I love and adore you all from my soul and my prayers are with you always

They call me Dominique Jones but I'm just God's angel

I love you all & God Bless!!!

www.ingramcontent.com/pod-product-compliance
Lightning Source LLC
Chambersburg PA
CBHW050552170426
43201CB00011B/1664